THE DRAFTSMAN'S HANDBOOK

Second Edition

L W Melville

LLB (Lond) Hons, PhD (Essex),
of the Middle Temple, Barrister at Law
(one-time member of the Society
of Public Teachers of Law)

LONGMAN

© L W Melville 1991

ISBN 0 85121 6900

First Edition 1985
Second Edition 1991

Published by
Longman Law, Tax and Finance
Longman Group UK Ltd
21–27 Lamb's Conduit Street
London WC1N 3NJ

Associated Offices
Australia, Hong Kong, Malaysia, Singapore, USA

A CIP catalogue record for this book is available from the British Library.

Phototypeset by Intype, London.
Printed and bound in Great Britain by
Biddles of Guildford Ltd, Surrey.

Contents

THE DRAFTSMAN'S HANDBOOK

UNIVERSITY OF
WOLVERHAMPTON

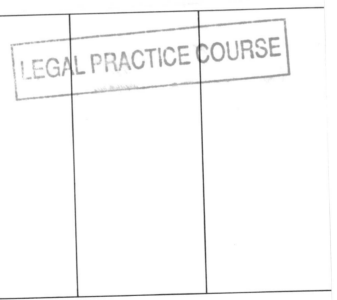

LEGAL PRACTICE COURSE

Please RETURN this item on or before the last date shown above.
Fines may be charged on overdue books.

WITHDRAWN

'Speech is civilisation itself'
Thomas Mann

'A word is the skin of a living thought—if one's thought is
non-existent or valueless, so will be the word itself'
Oliver Wendell Holmes

Preface

This book has its origins rooted in the preparation undertaken for a talk which I was asked to give at the Barbican Conference Centre, London in 1983. It was then that I realised that there was no booklet on the subject of drafting, for day to day consultation by the draftsman on any point of doubt.

George Coode of the Inner Temple wrote an erudite work in 1842, concerned primarily with the interpretation of statutes, and Lord Thring, chief parliamentary draftsman, produced a short pamphlet summarising the applied practices of the parliamentary draftsman's office in 1877. Other works have been published this century, yet I believe that what is offered here breaks fresh ground.

The first part of this work summarises the general principles of drafting with suitable examples or illustrations. The second part deals with the structure and composition of a clause, showing how a clause can be built up to requirements in stages. Part III is inspired by the belief that there is no substitute for the original sources. If one wishes to know how words that have caused particular difficulty were treated by the courts, then one must look to the judgments themselves, or at least extracts covering the essential passages. They are of crucial importance to the draftsman and for that reason call for full and careful treatment. Part III therefore consists of extracts from decisions of the courts. These verbatim extracts also provide good examples of the proper use of English. The fourth part brings together common legal terms which have been defined by statute and which need to be studied carefully on preparation of a draft document.

If one looks for a theme running through the matters dealt with in this work, one might conclude that the English like to keep their options open. Just as we are content to leave our Constitution unwritten, refuse to adopt a code of law (but instead rely on precedent so that old precedents can be discarded as new ones supplant their authority), so we refuse to adopt an academy of language to tell what words we may use and what we may not. Our language is a living abstraction ready to adopt new words as the occasion demands and to discard those that have served their purpose.

Part of this work also deals with the theme of 'plain English'. It is a feature of the 1990s that attention is being paid to plain English in legal documents. This is a subject worthy of some attention in its own right, since practically all documents prepared by lawyers, except pleadings, are for the benefit of the lay client, and he has a right to know and understand what is being put forward as applicable to him.

In the mid-1970s, some US states introduced statutory provision whereby the clarity of a document was to be taken into account before enforcement would be allowed. Attempts are being made to introduce a statutory requirement for clear and concise language in this country, and it is worth noting that Sir Ernest Gowers, anticipating the need for better English, in 1948 published his booklet 'Plain English'. This is a work still worthy of consultation in its latest edition as 'The Complete Plain Words' by Sir Bruce Fraser.

I must express my thanks to the editor of the *American Bar Association Journal* for permission to quote extracts from that Journal.

It is hoped that the reader will find that this booklet fulfils the purpose for which it is intended.

LWM
September 1991

Table of Cases

Table of Statutes

Introduction

'And books are yours within whose silent chambers treasure
lies preserved from age to age.'
                    Wordsworth, *The Excursion Book IV*

Sir Harold Kent, writing in his memoirs as Chief Parliamentary
Draftsman (*In On The Act*) gave a list of what he considered
were the qualities required of a parliamentary draftsman. Whilst
the conditions under which acts of Parliament are thrashed out
differ somewhat from those of a lawyer preparing an agreement
in his office, in that the former may find themselves having to
work all through the night if Parliament is sitting, whereas the
typical lawyer, though he may sometimes need to work late
hours, or at weekends, is rarely under the same pressure, yet
the qualities required of each appear to be much the same, and
for that reason would appear to be worth quoting. Sir Harold's
views may be summarised as follows:

(1) Intellectual capacity and intellectual stamina of a high
    order;
(2) A quick and retentive mind, because in any discussion
    of your draft you must be able to 'play it off the cuff
    and out of your head', and unless you can carry the
    substance and most of the detail in your mind, together
    with a knowledge of the relevant law, you 'haven't a
    hope';
(3) The ability to analyse a problem in depth so as to
    diagnose the provisions that are needed in the draft in
    relation to the subject matter;
(4) An imagination such as will enable you to project your-
    self into the situation that will come into operation
    when the draft is put into effect;
(5) A liking for this peculiar art, and a sense of dedication.

Much earlier, in the 1870s, Sir Henry Thring published a booklet on *Practical Legislation* in which he tells the novice that, when applying himself to the project, he should read through all the current acts of Parliament relevant to the subject, tying them together and reading the last first, working backwards. He is then to study a leading textbook on the matter followed by a reading of the leading cases, and having done that, he is told: 'A little practice, aided by an index of cases, will enable the student to complete his investigation very rapidly.' Hope springs eternal!

As to the interpretation of statutes it is worth noting what was said by Mackay in 1887, in the *Law Quarterly Review*, as to 'the great imperfection of English statutes' which he asserted 'is due not so much to the original drafting, which is very often the work of competent draftsmen, but to the machinery of parliamentary debate, through which their finished work has to pass, and out of which it often comes mangled so as to be unrecognisable by its author, and to become the butt for satire by cynical judges'. He rightly continues to assert that a good law should be capable of being understood by all persons of average intelligence, and urges that the draft should be in the hands of the original author. Unfortunately the latter suggestion is not practical for constitutional reasons.

In fact the difficulties facing the parliamentary draftsman are fully described by Sir George Engel in an article in the *Statute Law Review* for the Spring of 1983: anyone reading the article will cease to lay blame on those exercising the craft of parliamentary draftsman.

In a Code of Practice agreed between those representing publishers, and those representing authors it is stated that the publishing contract 'must be clear, unambiguous and comprehensive and must be honoured in both letter and spirit'. Fine words, which appear to assume that these goals have merely to be stated and they will be complied with. If that were true this book would not be necessary. The truth is that words are not scientifically limited in meaning like a mathematical equation. They are surrounded by an aura of uncertainty and controlled by context and circumstances. Drafting is partly a matter of an art but perhaps more of a science.

The essential purpose of a legal document is to avoid litigation in the event that a disagreement should arise later on. To endeavour to achieve certainty of meaning a document needs to be tailor-made to fit the parties' requirements, by a skilled person who can take the parties' legal measurements, cut the words to fit the pattern and sew it up with experience.

The principles applicable to the drafting of documents, and indeed the drafting of statutes or of pleadings, must be determined in the light of the rules applied by judges in their interpretation of material relevant to any litigation which comes before them. Whether the problem is as to the interpretation of an act of Parliament or of a document or pleading, the principles are sufficiently similar as to provide useful guidance on what to avoid and what to cherish.

The draftsman needs always to bear in mind those principles developed by the courts for construing commercial contracts. Briefly these are:

(1) The intention of the parties;
(2) The ordinary sense of the words;
(3) The construction of the document as a whole and the consistency in the use of language;
(4) Construction against the grantor – *contra proferentem*;
(5) The *ejusdem generis* rule;
(6) Implied terms;
(7) Uncertainty and statutory rules.

These principles are considered more fully in Chapter 3. They need to be balanced against the desirability for the document to be comprehensible to the client for whom it was prepared. The draftsman should always consider avoiding the use of long sentences whilst retaining the setting out of matters in detail.

Chapter 1

The English Language

'For a large class of cases . . . the meaning of a word is its use in the language.'
 Ludwig Wittgenstein, *Philosophical Investigations*

'What language is a system of, is signs.'
 Prof Barbara Strang, *Modern English Structure*

1.01 Importance of the study of language

Sir Francis Bacon is recorded as having made the remark: 'Men imagine that their minds have complete command of language; but it often happens that language bears rule over their minds.'

The relationship between thought, language and the real world has been the subject of many a philosophical study. The modern language philosopher, Ludwig Wittgenstein, at first took the view that language is essentially pictorial, but in his later view he regarded it as a publicly available social reality. However, as Gellner has pointed out in *Words & Things* to deify usage uncritically denies the value of reviewing usages as they arise and setting acceptable standards by those whose use of language is vital. There is no such thing as perfection in language.

Another aspect of the significance of language is expressed by Chomsky in *Cartesian Linguistics* thus:

It has always been clear that the normal everyday use of language involves intellectual abilities of the highest order. In view of the complexity of this achievement and its unique-ness to man, it is only natural to suppose that the study of language contributes significantly to our understanding of the nature of the human mind and its functioning.

4

Language is the lawyer's most important tool and it behoves him to know it well.

1.02 Origin of English

It is today difficult to tell what words can be traced back to original Indo-European, but English has words whose origin goes back to German, Scandinavian, Dutch, Anglo-Frisian, Saxon, and Celtic, as well as Latin and Greek. The Jutes, Angles and Saxons settled here in the fifth century bringing their languages with them, followed by the Vikings between the eighth and the tenth centuries. The early Roman invasion in AD 43 brought with it some contact with the Latin tongue, and later, with the coming of Latin speaking St Augustine in AD 597 and his preaching of Christianity, there was added a greater knowledge of that language.

These population movements are graphically illustrated in *The Times Atlas of World History* pp 98–101, and the situation as at AD 730 is described by the Venerable Bede in *The Ecclesiastical History of the English People*.

Finally, in the eleventh century, William the Conqueror landed with his entourage, speaking Norman-French amongst themselves, but the spread of the use of that language in this country was gradual.

A polyglot language cannot choose between different modes of inflexion and so it tends to discard all. That is what has happened, to some degree to the English language.

1.03 Roots of the Indo-European languages

The borrowing of words by one language from another is an inevitable process where two cultures meet. One of the most remarkable discoveries was made by Sir William Jones, a classical scholar and fluent linguist who was called to the Bar and who became a judge in Calcutta. Having a keen interest in Sanskrit, he was ideally placed to study it in depth. The result of that scholarship and research is worth repeating in his own words from the *Works of Sir William Jones*:

The Sanskrit language, whatever be its antiquity, is a wonderful structure; more perfect than the Greek, more copious than the Latin, and more exquisitely refined than either; yet bearing to both of them a strong affinity, both in the roots of verbs, and in the forms of grammar, than could possibly have been produced by accident; so strong indeed that no philologer could examine them all three without believing them to have sprung from some common source, which perhaps no longer exists. There is a similar reason, though not quite so forcible, for supposing that both Gothick and the Celtick, though blended with a very different idiom, had the same origin with Sanskrit; and the old Persian might be added to the same family.

1.04 Sloughing-off of inflexions

By the time of Chaucer (1340–1400), many of the various inflexions of English words, and the distinction of gender, which had been carried over from their numerous origins, had been shed. With their abandonment the beginnings of simplicity could be seen. As Potter writes in *Our Language*:

> English has surely gained everything and lost nothing by casting off this useless burden which all the other well-known languages of Europe still bear to their great disadvantage. How, we may ask, has English contrived to cast it off? Is there such a thing as 'the genius of the language'?

Clearly, he thinks that there is.

1.05 Effect of loss of inflexions

In an uninflected language the relationship between words, and consequently the meaning conveyed, becomes dependent upon their relative position in the word order. Syntax then becomes of the greatest importance, and this reliance upon syntax favours the short sentence. Long sentences need very careful structure and punctuation.

1.06 Use of English in the law

Alfred the Great (849–901) united the Saxon Kings to produce an early version of the common law, but from that time until well into the seventeenth century Alfred's English had to compete side by side with French and Latin. In 1362 the Statute of Pleading (36 Edw III c 15) required legal proceedings to be conducted in English, but it appears that commanding by statute the use of a particular language is hardly an effective way of bringing about a change in people's habits. It was necessary to repeat the command in the form of later acts requiring the use of English in legal matters in the time of Cromwell and again in George IV's reign. This is further explained in Holdsworth's *History of English Law*.

1.07 The language of Shakespeare

The Pilgrim Fathers took the language of Shakespeare with them to Virginia and Masachusetts in the early eighteenth century, and by the close of that century, when the Federal Constitution was ratified there were some four million English speaking inhabitants in that area. For the next half century, immigrants speaking a variety of European languages settled in that land, and later Chinese, Japanese and Africans arrived, but English prevailed. That may be some proof of its ready absorption, due perhaps to its structural simplicity, absence of inflexions, and reliance on little more than syntax for comprehensibility.

It is worth bearing in mind that Shakespeare's blank verse with its ten-syllable rhythm is considered to be the most natural form of speech. Sentences that have a multiple of ten syllables usually read well. If a sentence does not read well, it is worth trying out a ten-syllable or twenty-syllable form, but there is of course a limit to the use of that form, which, overdone, would lead to ridicule.

In 1783 Webster's *American Spelling Book* appeared, known in later editions as *Webster's Dictionary*. Webster set out to modify the spelling of certain words into simpler forms. It is the official government guide to spelling for the United States.

Today scientists and others engaged in technological and other such works on both sides of the Atlantic co-operate in the use of commonly spelt terms.

1.08 The quality of English: what is 'good English?'

Early attempts in this country to set up an 'academy of linguistics' as in France and Italy came to nothing, and in place thereof Dr Samuel Johnson produced his dictionary in 1755. The English approach was that, in the ultimate, attempts to fix a language for all time would bring greater loss than gain. Good English is a matter of usage from time to time.

Murray, an American who came to live in England, produced his grammar in 1795. Sweet produced, among other works, a masterpiece in 1898 devoted to that aspect of the language that contributes most to comprehensibility — syntax. The most respected work on the language came from the pen of Jespersen, a Dane, in seven volumes of which five deal with syntax. Jespersen regarded language as a growing phenomenon and English as a living language which had attained an advanced stage.

English was described in *The New English Dictionary on Historical Principles*, produced by Sir James Murray, and published in instalments from 1884 to 1928. It is now known as *The Oxford English Dictionary*. Murray was later assisted by others including Sir William Craigie, who helped in the writing of a corresponding work for America. *The Oxford English Dictionary* is the recognised authority for the British Commonwealth and the United States.

The Dictionary shows the origin of words in use in the main dialects from the year 1150 until the year 1500, after which dialectical expressions are omitted. It is the only dictionary in any language in the world which has such a wealth of information on a language and its origins. Its American counterpart in the form of *The Dictionary of American English on Historical Principles* was produced by Craigie and Hulbert in 1944.

The *Oxford English Dictionary* is used by the courts as an authority on language. This may be seen for example in the judgment of Maugham J in the case of *Re Cossentine* [1933] Ch 119 where the judge refers to the Dictionary for guidance on the meaning of the word 'between', and traces it back to Old and Middle English. He shows that its origin can be seen to spring from a word meaning 'two'.

1.09 Usage

In a living language its current form is a matter of usage. Recognition of this fact has given rise to books upon usage, of which one of the best known is Fowler's *Modern English Usage*, first produced in 1926, and subsequently revised by Gowers as a second edition in 1965. There is also a work *Usage and Abusage* by the New Zealand lecturer, Partridge, originally published in 1947 a sixth edition of which was published in 1965.

There are no absolutes in language, for though it strives to be a science, it is also tinged with artistry: we may say of something that it is 'partly true' ignoring the logic that a thing is either true or not; we say 'the very best' as though there were degrees of best; a thing may be said to be 'perfectly correct' notwithstanding that in logic it is either correct or not. These shades of meaning of words which appear to allow of no shading are recognised idioms.

As Strang puts it in *Modern English Structure*:

> If the rules set down in grammars and other linguistic studies have any validity, it is solely because they are accurate descriptions of the practices of the users of the language . . . If we consult grammars, dictionaries and handbooks of usage on particular linguistic questions, this is only as a short cut to usage itself, the only repository of authority. It has unhappily been the practice of many grammarians, especially in the last two centuries, to write of rules as if they had a source outside usage—in logic, in the nature of things in general, in authority—authority of other languages, past forms of the same language, the judgment and practice of eminent individuals, or God himself. This indefensible practice has brought the term rule itself into disrepute among linguistic scholars. In the sense we have used it, it remains useful: only we must be on our guard against assigning any prescriptive force to rules as we formulate them. They must be products of observation, not directives for behaviour. 'Doctors do not make the rules of health or of cell structure; they try to determine what these rules are and to come to terms with them'.

Jespersen, perhaps the greatest authority on syntax, uses throughout his work, as examples and illustrations of the points he makes, extracts from writers of distinction.

Chomsky looks towards a universal grammar whose principles embrace all languages. In his work *Aspects of the Theory of Syntax*, he writes:

> Observed use of Language . . . habits, and so on, may provide evidence as to the nature of this mental reality, but surely cannot constitute the actual subject matter of linguistics, if this is to be a serious discipline . . . The grammar of a particular language, then, is to be supplemented by a universal grammar that accommodates the creative aspect of language use, and expresses the deep-seated regularities which, being universal, are omitted from the grammar itself. Therefore it is quite proper for a grammar to discuss only exceptions and irregularities in any detail. It is only when supplemented by a universal grammar, that the grammar of a language provides a full account of the speaker-hearer's competence.

The study of language, in all its many aspects, has intensified remarkably in the second half of the twentieth century: the bibliography at the end of the book is a mere tiny sample of the vast output in this field.

1.10 Structure not grammar

Potter in *Language in the Modern World* claims that linguistics, the science of language, is 'on the way' to becoming an exact science. He writes:

> Structure, not grammar, is the key word to the new linguistics, just as, in a different way, it is the key word to modern mathematics and to nuclear physics. The scientific revolution of our time, in relativity, in quantum physics, and in biological statistics, has led to the reorganization of the logical structure of thought itself.

He continues with an admonition to acquire a sound knowledge of the mechanism of at least one other language as the best means of understanding the structure of English. The European languages are the most attractive for their utility, but a knowledge of Latin or Greek, or better still of Sanskrit, will offer a useful comparison. Indeed it was the work of Sir William Jones, and that of Friedrich von Schlegel *On the Language and Wisdom of the Indians* that prompted the study of comparative grammar, and this in turn led to the devising of structural linguistics.

1.11 Semantics and the meaning of meaning

This word 'semantics', and the alternative 'semasiology', are derived from a Greek word meaning 'significance' or 'to signify'. It is the science of the meaning of words.

Words can only have a meaning between those who are familiar with the words used. On seeing or hearing a word, it excites a response in the mind of the reader or listener with which he associates the phenomenon that the writer or speaker intended to invoke. It follows that to ensure that your meaning is conveyed, it is important to use familiar words unless there is a need to do otherwise.

It is not an exact science, for language does not have the exactitude of mathematics. Nevertheless Sir Ernest Gowers asserts in the first edition of *Plain Words* that 'Drafting is a science, not an art; it lies in the province of mathematics rather than of literature and its practice needs a long apprenticeship'. Note that he does not say that it is in the same league as mathematics, only that it 'lies in that province'.

1.12 The draftsman and the advocate

The lawyer's language in the court room will differ in many respects from that which he uses in his office when dictating letters or preparing drafts. For this reason as Justice George Rossman states in his article 'Better English for Lawyers as Draftsmen and Advocates' (48 Am Bar Assoc Jo 1048):

> —the lawyer who conducts both an office and a trial practice must learn two languages: the language of draftsmanship and the language of advocacy. A lawyer practices not only law but also the science of the correct use of language. We must not deceive ourselves into a belief that when we call in a stenographer, preparatory to the writing of a document or judicial opinion, the words will tumble out of our mouths without effort on our part. The capable preparation of any paper is an art: it requires effort, skill and training . . . In order to set forth with clarity the idea that he wishes to

express, the attorney must find the exact word that will call up in the mind of the reader the thought that he desires to impart. He must use as much care in his search for the right word as the painter uses in the selection of form and color . . . Just as the lawyer, upon drafting an instrument, may choose words that render the instrument invalid, so also he may select a word that will render it ambiguous and involve it in expensive, time-consuming litigation. For example, in an Arkansas case a will stated that all of the residue of the estate should be divided equally between the nephews and nieces upon the testator's wife's side of the family and his niece. The nephews and nieces upon the wife's side of the family were twenty-two in number; the husband had only one niece. The question was, should the estate be divided into twenty-three parts and one part be given to each niece and nephew, or should the wife's nieces and nephews receive one half and the husband's niece the other half. The draftsman of the will gave to its construer virtually no key that would enable him to penetrate the inner confines of the testator's intentions except the word 'between'. The dictionary told the court that 'between' signifies a division into two quantities for distribution to two persons or two groups. The court believed that if division into more than two parts had been intended the word 'among' would have been employed. It held that the wife's nieces and nephews should receive one half and the husband's niece the other half. Although the court's consultations of the dictionary did it credit, a leading text-book writer states that instruments affecting title seldom employ 'dictionary accuracy' . . . One can gain some conception of the volume of litigation which has its source in the failure of individuals to have chosen the right word by glancing at *Words and Phrases Judicially Defined*. Not every ill-chosen word there defined was written by a lawyer, but virtually every case there cited is an object lesson illustrating the need of having a person well versed in our native tongue and in the law of the land prepare all important documents. If our profession had a better command of our native tongue and wrote with clarity our legal papers, the volume of litigation would be reduced and some of the bitter feelings which are a by-product of litigation would not arise.

For reference purposes the bibliography contains an exhaustive list of UK legal dictionaries.

1.13 The aura of uncertainty

Dr Glanville Williams qualifies Gowers' statement that legal language has an affinity with mathematics in asserting that 'words have a penumbra of uncertainty'. He asserts this in the following passage from 'Language and the Law' (1945) 61 LQR 71:

> The lawyer, like the theologian, is faced with a number of texts that he regards as authoritative and that are supposed to settle any question that can conceivably arise. Each text was once drawn up by someone who presumably meant something by it; but once the document has left its author's hands it is the document that matters, not any unexpressed meaning that still remains in the author's mind. For the lawyer the words of the document are authoritative as words and there is no possibility of obtaining further information from the author either because the author is dead or because of the rules of evidence precluding reference to him.

Dr Williams is referring to those cases where the words or passages are not crystal clear, and few are. In other words, the meaning of a word will be determined in the ultimate by the context in which it occurs.

The reason why a semantic problem may arise over the use of a word lies largely in the practice of simile and metaphor. Indeed a very large part of our vocabulary consists in words which commenced as metaphors and have over the years been corrupted to a shorter form. The dangers posed by the use of metaphors are discussed in Chapter 6, para 6.08.

As an example of the 'penumbra of uncertainty' we may take a word that has been the subject of litigation in the House of Lords. It is derived from the root word 'traffic' and used in the Trade Marks Act 1938 in the phrase 'trafficking in a trade mark' where it occurs in s 28(6).

In the *Oxford English Dictionary* various applications of the word 'traffic' (in use soon after 1500 in various forms) are given including:

> 1. the transportation of merchandise for the purpose of trade; commerce; . . . b. a trading voyage or expedition; 2. (in the wider sense) the buying and selling or exchange of goods for profit; bargaining; c. (fig) 'surely this very traffics of faculties is that whereby we live . . .'; d. (with sinister or

evil connotation: Dealing or bargaining in something which should not be made the subject of trade) 'they make a Traffic of Honour and pay for it with fair words'.

This list continues in *The Oxford English Dictionary* to six sections.

The relevant section of the Act gives the Registrar power to refuse to register an agreement if he considers that the grant thereof 'would tend to facilitate trafficking in a trade mark'. It must have been a foregone conclusion therefore, in that milieu, that the word 'trafficking' would be construed in a pejorative sense, even though that is not the only meaning which may be ascribed to it. The courts did not find it possible to approve wholly of the way in which the applicants in *Re American Greetings Corpn's Application* [1984] 1 WLR 189 (HL(E)) were carrying on their business of dealing in a trade mark as a commodity in itself. The question then became one of fact whether the applicants' intention to treat the trade mark as a commodity in itself amounted to 'trafficking'. Holding that it did, the courts at the same time expressed the view that the law was somewhat outdated in the light of modern commercial practice in this field.

1.14 Syntax

We have seen from what has gone before, that in a fully inflected language, since the inflexions indicate the relationship of each word to the other, the order in which the words occur in a sentence is of little importance.

The reverse must, and does, hold true: that in a language with only a residue of inflexions, such as English, the order of words in the sentence is of the greatest importance in construing the meaning. It is referred to as 'syntax'.

(Those readers who write programs for computers will no doubt have met the warning notice thrown up occasionally by the operating system's program, 'syntax error'. There, the word syntax is being used in a broader sense to limit the number of error messages contained in the operating system's program and thereby save memory space. The fault in the entry may not necessarily be one of the wrong order of the elements of the program line, it may mean simply that something is missing, or some character is inappropriate.)

Whilst it is necessary, in a legal document, that the formal rules of grammar should be followed, it is clear that to attain as near to exactitude of meaning as possible, what really counts is the semantics of the words and the syntax of the sentence.

1.15 What is correct grammar?

The meaning of the word 'grammar' has changed over the years. Its early meaning was very general, relating to letters and literature. Its principal modern meaning, as given in *The Oxford English Dictionary*, is: 'That department of the study of a language which deals with its inflexional forms or other means of indicating the relations of words in the sentence, and with the rules for employing these in accordance with established usage'. Inflexions of words in English today are fortunately few and far between.

The rules of English grammar are essentially formal, and what the rules are is not agreed by everyone. To add to the problem, there are numerous idiomatic exceptions. Failure to observe the rules, however, whether from ignorance or for convenience, does not usually affect comprehensibility, and that is what really matters. Few would criticise the expression 'between you and I' yet, since a preposition should be followed by the accusative case, the 'I' should be 'me', but it is an accepted idiom in practice to adopt the former. Consider the example given us by no less a noble than the French Monarch Louis XIV in his famous utterance made as far back as the mid eighteenth century: 'L'Etat, c'est moi', thereby disobeying the rule that an intransitive verb, should be followed by the nominative case.

Arguably such exceptions are not true exceptions but examples of a subsidiary rule; that where emphasis is desired the accusative case after a transitive verb may be changed to the nominative, and in the case of an intransitive verb, to the accusative.

Let us bear in mind that there were no books on English grammar in Shakespeare's day.

Murray, an American who came to England and published

his famous book *Grammar in the English Language* in 1795, admitted in the Preface that 'When all is said, correct speech is less a matter of grammatical rule than of clear thinking'. So also Jespersen admits that language is not based on law, but on a set of human habits.

Logan Pearsall Smith, in his book on *Words and Idioms* has a very interesting passage dealing with the attack on the use of idioms, an extract from which follows:

> Is it not possible to maintain that these little irregularities which custom has accepted . . . have a certain value and vividness of their own which we might compare, perhaps to those slight irregularities and tiny flaws, which in the arts and handicrafts, in painting, sculpture, architecture . . . preserve some sense of the material employed—the stubborn material that, while it yields half-reluctantly to the form imposed upon it, still preserves some element, tenacious and untamed, of its original texture, quality and life? We have imposed our reason so rigorously upon the imagination, and all the unreasonableness of our human nature; the tendency of our language sets so strongly towards conformity of syntax, towards the mechanical, the monotonous, the trite; our speech, and above all, our writing, is so apt to run into uniform moulds of logical expression, that now and then a queer spelling, an anomalous plural, a blunder or hesitation, an irresponsible defiance of grammar or logic, awakens our attention—does it not—and conveys its meaning the more vividly by the very fact of its irregular form and appearance.
>
> Even the French purists of the seventeenth century . . . were still able . . . to recognize the charm of grammatical solecisms; the most eminent of them, Claude de Vaugelas, writing for instance, 'The beauty of language actually consists in this illogical way of speaking provided always that it is authorised by custom.' 'It is noteworthy,' he adds 'that all the ways of speaking which custom has established in contravention of the rules of grammar, should, far from being regarded as vicious, and as errors to be avoided, be on the contrary cherished as an adornment of language, which exists in all beautiful languages whether living or dead.'

Sir Ernest Gowers in the first edition of his book *Plain Words* devotes a chapter to a number of sometimes disputed grammatical rules, such as the split infinitive, the preposition at the end of a sentence, the unattached participle, the fused participle and the like. Since there is controversy over these features of our language, the choice of one form or another should not lead to serious consequences, and it may well be, for that reason, that Sir Bruce Fraser, in the latest edition of *The Complete Plain Words*, has omitted these chapters.

1.16 Style

Is style significant in a dry legal document? Is it not something applicable only to poetry or fine literature? The answer must depend upon the way in which one defines style. Contrary to what is thought to be the common attitude to style, it does not consist in flowery language, or in attempts to induce heightened emotional feelings.

J Middleton Murray in his booklet *The Problem of Style* expresses it in this way:

> I do not think that any one has ever more resolutely reduced the art of writing to essentials than Stendhal . . . He says in *Racine et Shakespeare*: 'Style is this: to add to a given thought all the circumstances fit to produce the whole effect that the thought ought to produce'.

In other words good style consists in precision, and is just as applicable to a legal document as to a poem, though the assessment of how precise is the thought to be conveyed by the words in each case, may call for different training or experience.

1.17 The two essentials to good English

By testing every sentence for the soundness of its syntax, and by the unhesitating use, where there is any doubt about the appropriateness of a word, of a thesaurus of synonyms so as to choose the most appropriate word, your English should be impeccable. Everyday rules of grammar, must, in legal text, be observed, notwithstanding anything in this work minimising its significance in attaining comprehensibility. As to the controversial grammatical rules, an intuitive selection of alternatives will normally suffice, but for those who value such rules, by all means be as punctilious as seems desirable, and if you can justify your choice by one of the books on usage, no one can criticise your writing. If necessary, consult also a Judicial Dictionary on any doubtful legal terminology.

It is not without significance that Medawar, in his book *Advice to a Young Scientist*, stresses the importance of intuition. Law is not so far removed from science, as not to call for similar advice. Not only is intuition likely to play a large part in your decision in which branch of the law to specialise, but also, if you have a legal problem to solve for a client, your decision as to what research, if any, is called for, will be largely a matter of intuition. So too, in your use of language for the purposes of your profession, intuition is a good guide if you have sufficient experience and sufficient desire to get it right.

Intuition is more than just common sense, though it is of the same order. It may be regarded as a personalised form of common sense, depending upon the amount of experience the individual in question has had in the subject matter, and the extent to which he has applied himself to problems and possibilities therein.

It may be of interest to note that in *A Theory of Justice*, John Rawls asserts that in looking for the elements of justice the use of intuition is the only satisfactory solution to solving the problems of, or selecting, the competing principles of justice.

Part I

Principles of Drafting

Chapter 2

The Function and Operation of a Document

Socrates to Hermogenes: 'Well, now, let me take an instance; suppose that I call a man a horse or a horse a man, you mean to say that a man will be rightly called a horse by me individually, and rightly called a man by the rest of the world; and a horse again would be rightly called a man by me and a horse by the world—that is your meaning?'

Dialogues of Plato (Cratylus)

2.01 Litigation

The perfect document will be filed away in a safe place and never looked at again; or if looked at will be found to dispose of any problem between the parties. For that is its function: to provide for possible problems in an agreed form in a language which brooks no argument.

It may be satisfactory to the lawyer on the winning side of any litigation that his document did not fail his client, but it is better if the document discourages litigation altogether.

2.02 The three graces

These are not Euphrosyne, Aglaia and Thalia, but Clarity, Conciseness and Comprehensibility. Unfortunately, these latter, which are those that concern the draftsman, are not fully reconcilable, and one has to perform a balancing act wherein comprehensibility is king and clarity queen; conciseness is merely a prince.

Sidney Parham Jr in his article on 'The Fundamentals of Legal Draftsmanship' (52 Am Bar Assoc Jo 831) asserts that:

> The goal of a legal draftsman is, by the nature of his craft, utilitarian rather than literary, but legal prose should be

polished as diligently and refined as fully as though the
goal were solely aesthetic. The draftsman's aims are clarity,
conciseness and comprehensive coverage rather than aesthetic beauty. All three are of primary importance, but the
first and last are essential to the utilitarian purposes of the
draftsman, while the second serves not only to further the
ultimate utilitarian purposes of clarity and comprehensive-
ness but to afford the only real opportunity available to the
practising attorney to exercise what literary talents he may
possess. . . . All three aims presuppose previous
thought. . . . The first step in draftsmanship is cerebration.
Until the draftsman has determined what he wants to say
and outlined in his mind the means of saying it, he has no
need for paper, pencil, the stenographer or the
dictaphone. . . . Brevity is not necessarily conciseness, and
a document should not be condemned because of its length
alone. Sometimes the comprehensive coverage required to
protect the client cannot be achieved without sacrificing
something in the way of brevity. Sometimes the demands
of clarity make length imperative. . . . If the language is
incomprehensible to the layman, the odds are that it will be
equally so to the professional. Even if this were not so, all
documents except pleadings are designed for the lay consumer and must be comprehensible to him.

Later in the same article, he makes the following points:

Like matters should be grouped together . . . semantics
seems to be the rock upon which the profession is commonly
accused of falling asunder, but no draftsman can hope to
achieve clarity without meticulous attention to his choice of
words. Words come in black, white and gray. The gray
words are the ones that create ambiguities. . . . You are not
expected to foresee the unforeseeable but to provide for
foreseeable possibilities.

Precision is the mark of good style, and precision often calls
for length. The Preface of *Forms and Agreements on Intellectual
Property and International Licensing* by the present author
includes the following remark in relation to clauses and agreements: 'Precision will be proportional to the length of the clause
(possibly in geometrical proportion)—the short, simple agreement so beloved of the business man being usually the least
satisfactory.'

It is a remark which perhaps calls for further explanation. By way of example, suppose you have lost your umbrella and you enquire at the lost property office or left luggage store, you will not get much response if you describe it simply as 'a black umbrella', but if you add that it is a short one you may halve the number of umbrellas to be searched; and if you mention that it also has a crooked handle you may halve that number yet again. Each additional qualification provides more precision to your description, and the effect is not unlike a geometrical progression.

The point to note is that each added description is of a different order from the earlier: elsewhere the use of a string of synonyms is criticised, here the reference is to a list of qualities, each of which is distinct from the other.

Consider the phrase 'the truth, the whole truth and nothing but the truth': the first reference to truth does not make the object of the phrase abundantly clear; though what is about to be given will be true, there may be part of the truth omitted, so we add the second phrase 'the whole truth', but in case something untrue were to be worked into the true, we add the third phrase to exclude it. Each phrase further narrows the preceding phrase.

Although the draftsman should aim for conciseness, clarity and comprehensibility often call for added non-synonymous matter to attain precision, and since precision is of paramount importance, it must prevail over conciseness.

2.03 Be consistent, use expertise but explain

It hardly needs to be said that terms that need to be repeated must be repeated by use of the same term, and in the same context. If the context is different the same term may be given a different meaning, as in the case of *Watson v Haggitt* [1928] AC 127 (PC). Here 'net profits' was held to have a different meaning when applied to the situation after the death of one of the partners, from that which it bore when they were both alive.

Remove anything that is seen ultimately to be redundant and avoid unnecessary repetition.

There are many usages found in legal documents arising in

the main from the cautionary practice of using both a word derived from the French and a word derived from the Anglo-Saxon, of which the following are a few examples where either word alone would suffice:

do and perform
good and effectual
goods and chattels
had and received
repair and make good
sell and assign
well and sufficiently

Avoid such unnecessary repetition. It is an entirely different case where more than one word is used and each is not a synonym; such use could be intended effectively further to modify the subject or predicate, and thus the meaning of the sentence, as exemplified above in relation to the description of a lost umbrella.

Words that have a specific legal meaning should be used where appropriate, notwithstanding that ideally your agreement should make sense to the lay client. Explain to him anything that needs explaining and let him have it in writing if necessary. All documents drawn by lawyers, other than pleadings, are drawn for the benefit of lay clients and should be comprehensible to them, even if only after concentrated reading.

2.04 Modernise

If a document is to function without criticism, the draftsman should consider whether the use of more modern language should be adopted.

There are a number of contemporaneous guides to the adoption of a more modern approach, following general dissatisfaction with the verbosity of earlier generations. The National Consumer Council has issued a number of guides dealing with relevant aspects of clarity for the benefit of the consumer, and they are worth studying: among these are *Plain English for Lawyers* and *Plain Words for Consumers*.

Certain time hallowed phrases used in legal documents are not readily discarded for something more up to date. The adoption of a more modern approach is a matter of individual decision, paying attention to what is seen to be acceptable. It is not without obvious danger where appropriate words or phrases have been judicially considered. An example of this is a phrase which has been condemned as inapt; the use of 'provided that' for what is in effect an exception or qualification of what precedes. A means of abandoning that phrase, is to start the first phrase with the qualification 'subject as hereinafter provided in the next following clause', which brings you back to the use of 'provided'. Thus, part of the well-worn phrase is justified, whilst at the same time a more modern approach can be made acceptable.

Another less objectionable, but sometimes criticised word is 'whereas' followed in subsequent paragraphs by 'and whereas'. The cure is simply to remove it without replacing it.

There are many other words which are inserted almost as a matter of habit, which can usually be removed, such as 'said', 'heretofore' and similar words added *ex abundanti cautela*, and which, when removed, are seen not to have played any essential part.

2.05 Construction of statutes; spirit or letter?; problems as danger signals

Chapter 5 deals with the interpretation and construction of documents: this Chapter deals with the anticipation of how a statute will be interpreted and applied to a document.

Whenever the validity or enforcement of a document depends on the provision of a statute, it is necessary to consider not only the provisions of the statute but also any decisions thereon; for this purpose a good textbook is needed.

In particular it is important to know whether the current line of decisions are hampered by a statute which has been interpreted literally to the dismay of some litigants, or whether it has been interpreted liberally and reasonably. Examples are given below of the literal interpretation adopted in construing s 35 of the Patents & Designs Act 1907, and it is a remarkable feature of this branch of the law, that although that section has since been twice re-enacted, no allowance for either of the decisions mentioned has been made, notwithstanding that each decision is open to pertinent criticism, as being interpretations which fail to take account of the spirit, intention or purpose of the section.

In such a case, it is desirable that a second opinion be obtained before the document is completed and put into force. An example of how a document can fail, through what seems to have been a reasonable assumption on the part of the legal advisers to the plaintiff, is provided by the decision in *Huntoon C v Kolynos (Inc)* [1930] Ch 528.

It appears from the report, which speaks of a 'licence deed' in relation to a patent, that the document was drafted by solicitors. A provision in the Patents & Designs Act 1907 which they had to take into account, intended to make void any provision in a contract relating to the working of the patent, which is likely to have the effect of widening the scope of the patent: thus you may not require that a licensee cannot exercise his licence unless, as a condition of working the patent, he acquires from you, the patentee, something which is not patented.

The patent related to a captive screw-on cap for a toothpaste tube. The essential point of novelty lay only in a length of spring wire which held the cap to the tube, the tube and its cap being well known. However, although the spring connector was apparently regarded as sufficiently novel, when applied to such an item, as to justify a patent, the patent granted was for the combination without any patent claim to any item singly. In a combination patent none of the items which make up the combination is separately protected, yet it is true to say in that case that without the connector, no patent would have been granted.

The arrangement agreed in the document had the advantage of not requiring the keeping and delivering of accounts of sales and payments of royalties, instead the patentee agreed to grant an exclusive licence to the licensee provided that the licensee obtained all his spring connectors from the patentee.

Did this arrangement fall within the prohibition of the Act? It was not against the spirit of the Act, for it was the essential item of the combination and apparently regarded as novel, and there was no allegation that an exorbitant price was demanded for the spring connectors. There was no earlier decision on the meaning of the relevant provision in the statute.

The Court of Appeal held the provision invalid, since the

patent was granted for the combination and the connector was not the subject of any patent claim—therefore it was something outside the patent. The effect of that decision was that the patentee had granted an exclusive licence gratuitously, since there was no other significant provision to his advantage in the document. It is a salutary tale of how a carefully prepared document may fail where the relevant law has not been tested in the courts, and where, perhaps, assumptions were made that proved wrong.

To underline the difficulty of statutes of this type, one has only to consider the case of *Tool Metal Mnfg Co Ltd v Tungsten Electric Co Ltd* [1955] 1 WLR 761 (HL), where the same statutory provision came under review in circumstances where the spirit of the Act was contravened, but technically it was held that the arrangement was not caught by the Act. There was no actual restriction imposed which extended the scope of the patent rights, but there was an inducement held out to the licensees to purchase their unpatented raw material from the patentee, on pain of loss of profit on any business done with unpatented raw materials obtained from other persons, beyond a quota, by the imposition of a penal royalty on such business.

2.06 Complex statutes

The constantly increasing number of statutes with which the lawyer needs to be familiar poses a heavy duty of care upon him or her to ensure the sufficiency and adequacy of documents in endeavouring to meet the requirements of the current statutory law. Unless great care is taken, not only to familiarise yourself with any statute that may be applicable to a case, but also with the decisions thereon, if there are any, there is a danger that the document will be found wanting if it has to be the subject of litigation. If there are no decided cases on the relevant points the situation is even more daunting.

By way of example, there are numerous decisions on the statutes dealing with the relationship of landlord and tenant, from which it is evident that considerable care and familiarity with the statutes and the current decisions, is vital if the document is to hold up in court in the way that your client wishes.

The omission of 'a' in a letting arrangement whereby premises were let to a college for the use of students, and which provided that they should be let 'as private residence only in the occupation of one person per room' was held not to be within the Rent Restriction Acts, since those Acts refer to 'let as a private dwelling' suggesting single occupation, and the 'a' was missing (*St Catherine's College v Dorling* [1980] 1 WLR 66 (CA)).

Similarly, the letting of two houses was held not to be within the Rent Restriction Acts since the Acts do not refer to letting in the plural (*Horford Investments Ltd v Lambert* [1976] Ch 39 (CA)). On the other hand, the subletting of furnished rooms, with the use of the kitchen in common with the tenant, has been held not to count as a 'separate' letting (*Baker v Turner* [1950] AC 401 (HL); and see *Goodrich v Paisner* [1957] AC 65 (HL)).

These are but a few examples of the traps into which one can fall without a thorough knowledge of the law applicable to a matter with which one may be concerned.

2.07 Acting on a personal misconstruction of a document

In *Re Allsop, Whittaker v Bamford* [1914] 1 Ch 1 (CA) a testatrix bequeathed property upon trust in favour of her nephews and nieces during their lives, and subject thereto on trust for their children 'who might be living at the time of the failure of the trust'. Upon the death of one of the nephews, the trustees, acting on erroneous legal advice, paid the income of the deceased nephew to his widow for the maintenance of her children. When this matter came before the court, it was held that the trust did not 'fail' until all the nephews and nieces had died.

In a case of this type one might criticise the use of the expression 'at the time of the failure of the trust' without making it clear what was meant by the phrase.

Chapter 3

Correspondence and Reports

'Manifesting one's thoughts by the voice with nouns and verbs, imagining the opinions of the mind in the stream which flows from the lips, as in a mirror.'

Dialogues of Plato, Theatetus

3.01 The letter writer

A lawyer may dictate forty letters a day, some of them quite lengthy. What style should he adopt, if any particular one?

There is as much need for comprehensibility, clarity and conciseness in a letter to a client as on a document. Unlike a document however, letters should be free from legal terms unless they are demanded by the matter being dealt with. The same warning against legal terms applies to the unnecessary use of Latin, or the abbreviations sometimes adopted in place of the name of the month ie inst, ult, prox. Use the month name, abbreviated if you must. 'Re' used in a heading to a letter is usually unnecessary when followed by the name of a matter in hand. In the text of a letter is it not better to say 'in regard to'?

In *The Complete Plain Words* Fraser suggests some foreign terms which should be discarded in favour of the English equivalent:

inter alia	among other things
per annum	a year
prima facie	at first sight
certeris paribus	other things being equal
mutatis mutandis	with the necessary changes made
carte blanche	blank cheque, or free hand

but he accepts that some foreign terms have become accepted

generally such as sub judice, fait accompli, and ad infinitum. It is a matter of judgment how this aspect of the language should be treated.

3.02 Be sparing of long letters

The client will not thank you for long explanations of legal niceties; nor indeed for long letters, if only because they suggest that the fee has been notched up too far on that account. Use short sentences and avoid long paragraphs. This is an aim worth bearing in mind.

3.03 Communication is the name of the game

The ability of the human being to communicate by language is a subject on which philosophers have, no doubt, pondered since time immemorial. The obvious has been discovered: that words only have meaning between those who understand the language being spoken at the level at which it is used. Hence your correspondence with your client must, if you are to make an effective impact and fulfil the client's needs, be on a level different from that used when communicating with other lawyers or experts.

3.04 The general tone

If you have the gift of putting into plain English what a lawyer would express in legal terms, use it every time you address a layman, whether in a letter or in conversation.

It is a matter of careful judgment whether the client should be addressed as a personal friend. The safe course is to be neutral without being formal, whether addressed by first name or surname.

An over-familiar tone in your correspondence (or indeed in conversation), even perhaps, when writing to a personal friend, will detract from the sense of dealing with an expert, which is what the client is expecting, with the consequence that the recipient may begin to question whether he has chosen the right adviser.

3.05 The voice of experience

Just as a medical man is supposed to be able to put on a 'bedside manner', so a lawyer should be able to speak with the voice of experience.

A client should not be required to pay fees except for expertise which he himself cannot exercise. It should be apparent to him, from any conversation and the tone and structure of any correspondence, that the man he has chosen has the expertise. The lawyer should have the knowledge to deal with the matter he has accepted, even though he may need to refresh his memory for want of a recent case. If the facts are rare, that much may be admitted, but they must be truly rare.

At the same time allowance must be made for what you cannot know: to pretend to be able to predict how a judge will decide a case is to invite disaster. A point of law that has never been settled, may properly be admitted as a matter for a personal judgment, pointing out that it is a personal judgment, that may prove to be wrong.

3.06 Reports

When preparing a report, such as a statement of a witness, it is a mistake to insist on the verbatim unless there is a compelling reason to the contrary. Convert the witness's words into good English, suitably paragaphed if necessary, and repeat your corrected form to him to get his confirmation that that is what he really means.

3.07 Brief to counsel

A brief to counsel calls for the use of good, clear and comprehensive English. In such a document one may be as full and comprehensive as seems appropriate in order that no point may be missed. The expected arguments of the opposition should be anticipated and commented upon briefly.

3.08 Non-legal English

In correspondence and reports it is recommended that terminology which has an essential legal connotation should not be used unless there is no satisfactory alternative. The reason should be clear; certainly in letters to a client, or indeed to third parties except perhaps other lawyers, the need to use familiar terms is an essential policy to adopt if you are to convey precisely what you have in mind.

3.09 Word watching

In using non-legal English it is well worthwhile looking out for clichés and overworked metaphors, and then searching for a more appropriate word or phrase. Some of the more common are listed in para 3.01 above and will be found dealt with fully in *The Complete Plain Words*.

3.10 Good style

Business letters or reports do not have to be literary master-pieces, but the man who is familiar with the best of literature will write a more effective letter than the one who is not.

It is well worthwhile endeavouring to adopt a good clear style of writing, and a few points may therefore not be out of place:

(1) Make free use of dictionaries, Thesauri of synonyms and antonyms, Fowler's *Modern English Usage*, and other such compendia of everyday information and practice.

(2) Be concise and avoid repetition.

(3) Use analogies if they will help explain a point.

(4) Use similes and metaphors, so long as they are well chosen, the better to explain something which the addressee might find difficult.

(5) Get your punctuation right.

(6) Vary the length of your sentences.

(7) Take care that your verbs are conjugated according to whether you are using the singular or the plural. At the same time allow for plural words treated as singular and vice versa: use the singular after 'none'. Use the possessive case with the gerund.

(9) Take care with 'that' and 'which': both in not failing to use them where appropriate, and using the right one in the right place. Where they are considered to

be interchangeable, 'that' should be preferred to 'which'. Fowler says that 'that' should be used in relation to things or people that are defined or limited, and 'which' when there is no such definition or limitation.

(10) Do not allow so-called rules of grammar to interfere with the clarity of your language. Thus, there is said to be a rule that one must not split an infinitive, yet, as Jespersen has pointed out in *Analytic Syntax*, in the phrase 'a vicious backhander which I failed to entirely avoid', not to split the infinitive would produce a change of meaning ie the sentence would then end 'I failed entirely to avoid'. The first version means that the back-hander made some impression, whereas the second means that it struck home with force.

Chapter 4

Stages in the Preparation of a Document

'I—this thought which is called I—is the mould into which the world is poured like melted wax.'

Emerson, *The Transcendentalist*

4.01 Taking instructions

This chapter is concerned with the making of a mould in the form of an agreement into which words are to be poured. The result has a permanency somewhat greater than wax. There must therefore be an endeavour to ensure that the mould is right and that the words are appropriate.

There is no golden rule on how to go about taking instructions from a client who seeks advice on a business matter involving legal drafting. It will to some extent be determined by the standing of the client—whether he has had experience of entering into legal transactions or not.

If in any doubt, always assume that he does not know what information you will need and question him thoroughly until you are reasonably satisfied that you have the basis of a possible business arrangement.

If he is an employee, make sure that he has the necessary authority to give you instructions.

There is no need to insist on the client's coming to your office for the purpose, if it is more convenient to him for you to go to his business premises, or some site where the project is to be initiated. If the first contact is to be somewhere other than premises where notes can readily be made, take a portable tape recorder with you—using it openly of course—as a means of reminding you of the essential details discussed.

4.02 Visiting the locus quo

One reason why the Duke of Wellington never lost a battle lay no doubt in his habit of seeing for himself: 'I will get upon my horse, take a look and then give you my opinion' was the substance of his usual reply when asked an opinion. Incidentally he also claimed to be 'the best read man in England', an attainment which all lawyers might strive towards, even if the reading was limited to the books that deal with a particular speciality.

Where your instructions relate to an operation at a factory, or other business premises, particularly if the business has anything unusual about it, it is often well worthwhile visiting the premises and seeing what goes on. It is a matter for you to judge whether it appears that such a journey may be justified, but since you will be charging the client for your time in travelling and working at his premises, you should seek his views and co-operation. Take full advantage of any opportunity to see for yourself what goes on in practice. However thoroughly you question a client about the proposed transaction, you may still find something which the client did not realise ought to be dealt with in the documents.

4.03 Get it into writing

As soon as the essentials are known get them down in summary form, let your client have a copy, and seek his confirmation that your understanding is correct.

Decide how the parties are to be referred to. It is best to use designations which indicate the role each party plays, such as Vendor and Purchaser, Grantor and Grantee, Manufacturer and Distributor, Principal and Agent. Avoid 'party of the first part' etc, in case you get the numbers mixed. Surnames 'without handles' such as 'Smith', 'Brown' etc are unnecessarily crude.

Use the chosen designations in your summary so that the client can see what is proposed.

4.04 The first step—a 'good think'

Before attempting the first draft it is helpful to apply your mind to the intended contents, and endeavour to envisage mentally what will be included and in what order. Then set down the order of the intended contents and the headings to be used for each clause. Time spent in contemplation is not likely to be wasted—study your notes and if in doubt try alternatives until you are satisfied that your outline is right.

4.05 Research the law

Apply your mind to the possibility that there may be legal restrictions on what is permissible in the particular case: the most common are matters relating to taxation, company law, restrictive trade practices or European Antitrust law (arts 85 and 86 of the Treaty of Rome in particular). Satisfy yourself on these points before starting on a drafting exercise. Get the essential points clearly in your memory for reasons stated below in para 4.13.

Consult the leading textbooks, and having found a point that needs to be considered, go to the original sources ie the decisions of the courts, and read the judgments, and perhaps the arguments as well if they are also reported. No research which fails to go back to the original sources is ever safe. It is for that reason that there are included in Part III extracts from decisions on matters of general interest.

4.06 The first draft

The ideal method of preparing a first draft is to put an 'engaged' sign on your door, tell the telephonist not to disturb you, take a pen, sit down comfortably and write the draft out by hand.

Even if you use ready-made clauses from a precedent book, there is much to be said for copying out the chosen clause in your own handwriting, and choosing your own style and content as you read through it.

Why this insistence on handwriting? In the first place, it forces you to consider each word as you proceed; secondly you can see the draft emerging as you go along; thirdly you can break off at any time if, for example, you realise that there is a point that needs further investigation. The alternative of dictating into a tape recorder does not allow you to see what you are producing, and of dictating to a secretary may cause you to hesitate before breaking off, since another person's time will be wasted while you look up the point. Justice George Rossman, of the Supreme Court of Oregon, in recommending the use of hand-writing wrote:

> Unfortunately, the idle stenographer who is sitting by and who is receiving no dictation while we are puzzled over the needed word may cause us to terminate our search too soon. All important papers should be written by hand before they are dictated. Very likely the absence of the typewriter in the days when our nation's great state papers were prepared by our early brethren at the Bar may account for their excellence ('The Lawyer's English' 48 Am Bar Assoc Jo 50).

4.07 Definitions

Sir Henry Thring (later Lord Thring) who was Chief Parliamentary Draftsman in the 1870s, wrote a small booklet on the drafting of acts of Parliament entitled *Practical Legislation* (HMSO 1877). It was based on a collection of memoranda that had previously circulated in the office dealing with various points of practice.

He makes two points on the matter of definitions. The first is that definitions should always be consistent with the matter defined eg the definition of 'piracy' should not be such as to include 'mutiny'. The second point is of some passing interest; whilst he concedes that logically definitions should be placed at the beginning of an act, (because the reader will not be able to understand the act until he is master of the definitions), he then makes the point that in the case of acts of Parliament, politically their proper place is at the end of the act. A definition frequently narrows or widens the whole scope of the act, and Parliament cannot possibly judge whether such narrowing or widening is expedient until they have become acquainted with the act itself. Readers will be aware of the continued practice of placing definitions at the end of an act of Parliament. That is surely a special case: when members of Parliament consider a bill it will be their first sight of it, and there is no doubt an established practice of going through a bill clause by clause.

On the matter of definitions then, which plays a very important role in drafting, the advice offered here is to draw them up on a separate sheet or sheets and have the list available as you proceed to draft the document. From time to time you may find that you need to amend a definition, or add another. As to its ultimate position in the draft, put it at the beginning. Those concerned to read it will be familiar with the substance; moreover, if they wish, they can skip the definitions and read them later.

4.08 Mark and date each version of the draft

Every printed version of the draft terms should carry at the top left-hand corner the number of the draft, your initials, and the date the draft was completed, thus: DRAFT 1/ABC/84–04–01. The date as shown refers to year, month and day in that sequence but you may of course adopt such other sequence as you please, so long as it is uniform and known to your staff. If a wordprocessor is used, do not forget to add the disk number and file reference.

If the draft extends to more than one sheet the sheets should be securely held together—not with sliding clips, but with metal fasteners which penetrate the corner of each sheet. Better still is to use a stapling machine along the left-hand edge several times so that the draft opens in book form.

4.09 Use of wordprocessor

A wordprocessor is an excellent alternative to handwriting if you will personally operate it and key in the text: the parallel is obvious. If however you have a stored data bank of precedents, they should be treated like any other ready-made precedents; carefully considered word by word and adapted as necessary.

4.10 Photocopy, cut and paste, then rephotocopy

If you are intent on using previous drafts or precedents but wish to be selective, and you take photocopies of the selected pages or clauses, cut out what you want, mount on scrap and photocopy; you will have a draft of sorts which will need to be retyped. It should also be carefully scrutinised word by word to ensure that it fits the particular requirements.

4.11 Books of precedents

Books of precedents are invaluable as reminders of what is commonly used, but it is unwise to think that any of the precedents are likely to be useable exactly as they appear. They are useful checklists, and the clauses may help you devise what you need for a particular case. Always read any clause very carefully before adopting it without any change. Better still, write it out by hand, making amendments as you go. Indeed it is a good practice to endeavour to rephrase the clause before adopting it, so long as the new version is at least equal to or better than the original copied.

It is salutary to note the judicial notice taken of precedents as when the perpetuity rule was overlooked in *Dunn v Blackdown Properties Ltd* [1961] Ch 433. Two plots of land which abutted on a private road known as Pine Tree Hill, were conveyed to the plaintiffs' predecessors in 1926 and 1938 respectively. There was included in the conveyances a right to use the sewers and drain, now passing or hereafter to pass, under the private road, the latter belonging to the defendants' predecessors.

The defendants' predecessors in title constructed sewers for surface water and for soil respectively and these passed under the private road.

The plaintiff, successor in title to the plots, claimed a declaration that she was entitled to have the premises connected to those sewers.

Cross J at p 437: 'The plaintiff does not at present need any drainage facilities over Pine Tree Hill, but she claims that she has a right to connect the drains from any houses which she may hereafter build on the pink or blue land with any sewers belonging to the defendants or their successors in title which may then be in Pine Tree Hill, and in particular with the soil sewer. In answer to that claim the defendants pleaded:

(1) that . . . the respective grants were void as infringing the rule against perpetuities, and, alternatively

(2) that the plaintiff is not entitled to use any part of the sewers and drains passing under other parts of the defendants' land in respect of which the plaintiff has no right of drainage.

Subject to . . . s 162 Law of Property Act 1925 . . . there is no doubt that the rule against perpetuities applies to grants of easements. It follows that where the grant is not immediate but is of an easement to arise in the future it will be void unless it is limited to take effect only within the perpetuity period.

It is not however always easy to decide whether the grant in question is of an immediate right or of a right to arise in the future. . . . If there had been a sewer under Pine Tree Hill at the dates of the grants to her predecessors in title the plaintiff could have claimed . . . that the owners of the pink and blue land had from the first a right exerciseable at any time to make connections with and use that sewer. . . . It is not for the owners of the pink or blue land to decide whether or not a sewer will or will not pass under the road in future. That is for the owners of the road to decide, and I do not see how this part of the right granted can be treated as anything but the grant of an easement to arise at an uncertain date in the future. . . . In the ordinary case, which the forms in the books of precedents have in mind, one has a row of houses adjoining a street and a sewer running under the whole length of the street. The words used there are not designed to meet a case such as the present. . . .

In the result I hold that the action fails on this question.'

4.12 Style and appearance

A document should be easy to read, and one of the features which aids easy reading is the physical layout of the text. Use wide margins both at the top and bottom of the page as well as down each side—any extra cost of paper is well repaid.

Give every clause an appropriate heading which describes succinctly what it is about.

Add marginal notes indicating the function of the clause. This is useful especially in the case of a long document, or a document which necessarily has lengthy clauses.

Separate the clauses from each other with an extra lineal space so that each is distinct from the other.

Number the clauses and subclauses and put the numbers in the margin so that they are easily picked up.

Another useful feature which improves appearance is to surround the text on each page with heavy ink lines along the margins and across the top and bottom; use double lines so long as they are neatly parallel and equally spaced.

Attach a front sheet which lists the clauses and operates as an index.

4.13 Sleep on it

Ideally, when the first draft has been prepared—even if it was prepared painstakingly—it is well worthwhile, if time does not press too hard, to put it away for twenty-four hours. The contents are stored in your mind, and the mind has the facility to review subconsciously what it holds. It seems that the subconscious is self-activated and will seek answers to questions that have remained unanswered, and send to the conscious mind notification of inconsistencies lying in memory.

A day later, taking your draft out of the cabinet and looking at it, you must not be surprised if fresh ideas for improvement spring to mind straight away. It can and does happen. Herbert Spencer remarks on this facility in his *Autobiography*:

It has never been my way to set before myself a problem and puzzle out an answer. The conclusions at which I have from time to time arrived, have not been arrived at as solutions of questions raised; but have been arrived at unawares—each as the ultimate outcome of a body of thoughts which slowly grew from a germ. Some direct observation, or some fact met with in reading, would dwell with me: apparently because I had a sense of its significance. It was not that there arose a distinct consciousness of its general meaning; but rather that there was a kind of instinctive interest in those facts which have general meanings . . .

I give this explanation, partly to introduce the opinion that a solution reached in the way described, is more likely to be true than one reached in pursuance of a determined effort to find a solution. The determined effort causes perversion of thought. When endeavouring to recollect some name or thing which has been forgotten, it frequently happens that the name or thing sought will not arise in consciousness; but when attention is relaxed, the missing name or thing often suggests itself. While thought continues to be forced down certain wrong turnings which had originally been taken, the search is vain; but with the cessation of strain the true association of ideas has an opportunity of

asserting itself. And, similarly, it may be that while an effort
to arrive forthwith at some answer to a problem, acts as a
distorting factor in consciousness and causes error, a quiet
contemplation of the problem from time to time, allows
those proclivities of thought which have probably been
caused unawares by experiences, to make themselves felt,
and to guide the mind to the right conclusion.

What is perhaps equally important is the review of the law
in conjunction with the preparation of the draft: the mind, in
reviewing recent contents impressed upon it, has the facility for
marrying up the various items and noticing discrepancies if they
exist. That is one of the reasons which justifies your reminding
yourself of the applicable law in conjunction with the preparation of the draft, and then leaving the matter for a reasonable
period, preferably overnight.

4.14 Amendment

There is a difference of practice on the matter of amendments
to be made to a draft document by 'the other side', according
to whether it is a conveyancing matter or not. The Conveyancer
uses coloured inks to show proposed changes, leaving the original text as it is, and there is a convention on the matter of
which colours to use for each successive amendment to the same
passage, or indeed a fresh amendment. Apart from amendment
to pleadings in litigation, with which this work is not concerned,
and conveyancing, amendment in these days of the photocopier,
is by way of redrafting and supplying a new amended draft
showing the date of its preparation. Thus, after the first amendment each party will hold two drafts, the original and the amended version, which may be replaced with a third redraft suitably
dated and so on. This leads to a great deal of accumulated
drafts, each of which should be retained until the matter is
complete. At the same time the text is more easily compre-
hended without being cluttered with earlier amendments subsequently crossed out.

In practical terms, to effect an amendment, the original copy
is photocopied, the original filed away for archival purposes,
and the photocopy used for amendment. This may well be done
in handwriting in the first instance, and then the computer-

stored copy is amended accordingly and an amended copy printed on the computer printer. Always print and store a hard copy of a draft prepared on a word processor, and reprint when the data is amended.

4.15 Revision

When revising a draft prior to resubmission to the other party, or prior to engrossment, an important task is to scan each sentence to satisfy yourself that the syntax is sound, ie that the word order renders the sentence as clear as practicable. On this point see paras 1.10–1.13 above.

4.16 The final 'engrossment'

Although it is not nowadays the practice to 'engross' an agreement on vellum, parchment or imitation versions of those ancient materials, it is not uncommon still to refer to the final copy as the 'engrossment'. A more modern term is the 'signature copy'.

If there is time to 'sleep on' what is regarded as the final copy, do so—you may think of a good last point.

Have the final copies bound in one of the various ways known in the profession; use the traditional green silk tape to sew down one edge with the ends sealed with sealing wax, or use a binding machine. Whichever method is used, take care to see that all the pages of the document are securely held together and in the correct order.

4.17 Signature and date

In a straightforward case a document will become effective from the date entered in it. If all parties are present together on the day when it is intended to come into effect, and they execute it there and then, there will be no problem.

Life is not like that: usually there will be duplicate signature copies and each of the parties will decide when to execute them in their own or their solicitors' offices. If they have not been advised about dating, they may or may not enter the date of execution as the day of signature. For the above reasons it is advisable to agree beforehand on the date of commencement, and enter it in the document as such. The actual date of signature is then not important, but each signature copy must bear the same date. In the case of a limited company using its seal there will be an entry in the minute book of the authorisation of the sealing.

Where practicable the signing of a document should be supervised by the legal adviser to ensure that it is properly signed by an authorised person, and witnessed if necessary.

Although it is not usual to show the actual date of signature of each of the parties signing, there is no objection to it so long as the date of commencement is clearly stated in the document. An expressly stated date of commencement is particularly important if dates of actual signature are to be given and they do not coincide.

Consider the question whether the document carries a liability to inland revenue stamp duty.

4.18 Authorisation of signature

Where the parties are partnerships, limited companies, friendly societies, co-operatives, charities and the like, some attention should be paid to the office held by the signatories. Satisfy yourself, in writing if thought desirable, that the signatories have the power to bind the parties that they represent to that type of document.

4.19 Delivery of sealed document

Where a company properly executes and seals a document, it may be deemed to have been 'delivered', in the sense that it becomes binding and cannot be revoked by refusing to hand it over in return for the counterpart executed by the other party (*Beesly v Hallwood Estates Ltd* [1961] Ch 105 (CA)). It will be a question of fact whether it was delivered unconditionally or in escrow. As to execution of instruments by a UK corporation see s 74 of the Law of Property Act 1925.

There are decisions made at the time of Elizabeth I which may still be quoted as to the manner of execution of a deed at common law. A date is not essential to a deed; its date in law will be the date when it was delivered. Thus in one case, a deceased had executed and delivered a deed which at the time had no date; later a date was inserted which was after the date of his death: it was held that the deed was good and that its date was the date of delivery. The reason for this rule concerning the date is that since the delivery is made after the deed has been executed, the true date cannot be entered before delivery has been effected (*Goddard's case, Goddard v Denton* (1584) 2 Co Rep 4b; *Dodson v Kayes* (1610) Yelv 193; *Doe d, Whatley v Telling* (1802) 2 East 257; *Hall v Cazenove* (1804) 4 East 477).

4.20 Amending a draft

(1) Amendments should be obvious

It is vital, when acting in a matter involving another party represented by his own lawyer, that in making amendments to a draft which has been brought into existence for the matter being dealt with, and a copy has been provided to the other side, for each party to be able to see clearly what amendments have been made without obscuring the text being amended. With the advent of computers there has been an abandonment of the use of coloured inks to indicate the amendments desired, and by which side the amendment has been made, and this gives rise to the problem of indicating what amendments have been made by each party.

To send a retyped or reprinted draft without showing what amendments, or further amendments, have been made is disconcerting to the other party, quite apart from obliging him, or an assistant, to spend time making comparisons to discern the changes. It then becomes necessary to mark the reprint in a manner which will show what the amendments are, or to mark the changes by hand so that the other side's attention is drawn to them, and for each party to show the date of each of his amendments.

Consider, in any new matter, whether the old practice of using coloured inks is appropriate: it may still be found useful in some cases. When the available colours have been exhausted, a new draft is justified.

(2) Amendments not previously agreed

Consider carefully when making amendments not previously agreed; there are those who object to the practice unless the other party's attention is drawn to the desired amendment.

(3) Use of computers

Where a computer is used for the composition of the text, there are advantages in submitting a disk with the printout, with the intention and understanding that your correspondent may make a copy for his own use, and will, if he wishes to make further amendments, return the disk with the program amended. It is helpful if each party can use a different typeface. Since this practice may not be fully accepted in some cases it is desirable to ascertain the view of the other party.

(4) Amend only on matters of substance

Amendments should not be made on semantic grounds: confine amendments to matters of substance. Thus, if the terms 'landlord' and 'tenant' have been used there is usually no point in changing those designations to 'lessor' and 'lessee'.

(5) Where several documents are involved

Where there is more than one document in a transaction, and one of the documents is to be altered, be careful to look for consequential amendments to the other documents.

(6) Mathematical calculations

Where mathematical calculations are involved (eg in a licence to quarry gravel where the licensee is to pay according to the quantity extracted) there is no objection to the use of an algebraic formula, but it adviseable to accompany the equation with a textual version of the formula ('spell it out in words'). Use care in drafting the linguistic version of the formula.

(7) Appropriateness of the proposed matter

Although you will be acting on instructions received, one should ask oneself whether the transaction as conceived by the client is the most appropriate structure to achieve the intended result or relationship. Make sure you fully understand all the relevant facts together with the parties' intentions, and, in the light of your legal knowledge and experience, consider whether the matter could be more advantageously arranged or structured.

(8) Apply your mind to possible pitfalls

Do not forget such rules as the rule against perpetuities and the like.

(9) Consider the effect of the exercise of any ongoing provisions

Do not make the mistake of granting a lease with an option to renew without providing that the new lease will exclude the option, otherwise you will have produced an unintended perpetuity (which will be invalid).

(10) Create a master file of sample drafts

It is particularly helpful to have ready access to earlier work when receiving similar instructions in a later matter. Create a master file of the various transactions in which you become involved for possible further use as guides to another transaction of similar character, as a comparison. Consulting your master file for a new matter puts you on the track for another transaction which has similar features. Consulting it prior to taking instructions in a similar matter should ensure that you do not forget to ask all the right questions. If the draft is on a disk the draft should be marked to indicate on what disk it is written.

(11) Training for modern technology

Modern technology calls for proper training of all staff, whether principals, assistants or secretaries, in order that everyone may make the best and most cost-efficient use of their equipment, time and expertise.

(12) Available statutory provisions

Take advantage of those statutory or other official rules and orders which provide standard clauses in any matter under consideration. For example, the use of the well-known term 'beneficial owner' carries with it a statutory effect and saves having to determine what is appropriate and then composing it: the statute should satisfy, but make sure that the one chosen does so satisfy by checking.

(13) Use of printed forms

Use stationers' printed forms where available, eg where an enduring power of attorney is called for, and adopt an appropriate legislative provision based upon the current statute which will normally contain explanatory notes.

Chapter 5

Interpretation and Enforcement

'Words are the tools and subject matter of lawyers.'
Lord Simon, *Hensher (George)* v *Restawile Upholstery (Lancs)* [1976] AC 64 (HL)

'For strangely in this so solid-seeming World, which nevertheless is in continual restless flux, it is appointed that sound, to appearance the most fleeting, should be the most continuing of all things.'

Carlyle, *Sartor Resartus*

5.01 Proper law

In this work it is assumed that the document will be governed by English law. That may not be so if you are contracting with another party in another country, who may have enough 'muscle' to require that the law of his country shall govern the matter. If that happens your draft ought to be checked by a lawyer in that country.

5.02 Interpretation

Where a document has to be enforced by legal action the court will, in interpreting the document, limit its view of the matter by the words actually used in the document; extrinsic evidence that the meaning or intention was other than that expressed in the document cannot be adduced, unless some part of the contents, or the surrounding circumstances in which the contract was made, show that there is an ambiguity between the intentions and the words used.

There is no paramount rule of good faith in English law, allowing evidence of intention arising from the negotiations:

49

only where it is clear that one party was endeavouring to take advantage of a known mistake, will the law consider the surrounding circumstances. Thus where a landlord failed to provide, as he intended to do, unknown to the other party, that the lessee should bear part of the cost of structural repairs, the court refused to allow rectification of the lease (*Riverplate Properties Ltd v Paul* [1975] Ch 133 (CA)).

Again, in *Watson v Haggitt* [1928] AC 127 (PC) where a partnership agreement between two partners provided that on the death of a partner, his estate was to be paid a one-third share of the net profits for five years, the court refused to interpret 'net profits' on the same basis as it had been interpreted when both partners were alive, ie deducting a 'salary' paid to each, before dividing profits; for there could be no salary to a dead partner. Therefore it was held that 'net profits' had a different meaning after a death, requiring that the one-third share be taken out of the profits before the surviving partner deducted his 'salary'.

5.03 Mistake

Where it appears from the facts that there is some ambiguity between the parties' intentions and the recording of the arrangement, the document will be construed against the factual matrix surrounding the negotiations leading up to the conclusion of the transaction (*Hyundai Shipbuilding & Heavy Industries Co Ltd v Pournaras* [1978] 2 Lloyd's Rep 502 (CA)). The essential purpose of interpretation is to ascertain what it was that each of the parties intended to accomplish by means of the document.

In *Scriven Bros & Co v Hindley & Co* [1913] 3 KB 564 the court found itself unable to interpret the document as a binding contract: a party bidding for tow genuinely thought it was hemp and in consequence bid an unduly high price, the auctioneer thinking that he was unfamiliar with the market. The court was in the same position in *Raffles v Wichelhaus* (1984) 2 H & C 906 where the contract referred to goods on a named ship, but unknown to each of the parties each was thinking of a different ship of the same name.

The court will not allow one party to take advantage of an obvious mistake of the other party, where the other party clearly is unaware of his mistake; as in *Hartog v Colin & Shields* [1939] 3 All ER 566 where a contract, having been negotiated on the basis of a purchase of animal skins at so much per pound, (a pound representing approximately three pieces), was written in the form of a price per piece, making the whole transaction uneconomic to the obvious knowledge of the vendor.

5.04 Words and figures

Generally words will prevail over figures unless they are inconsistent, in which case it has been held that the second of the two expressions will prevail (*Re Hammond, Hammond v Treharne* [1938] 3 All ER 308). It is clearly preferable to use words, but if figures must be used, check them and rely on the figures without words.

5.05 Construction

After the court is satisfied about the manner in which the document is to be interpreted, it then turns its attentions to the effect of the document as a matter of law. This is known as construing the document, so as to see whether the intentions of the parties, ascertained by interpretation, can be enforced in the light of the governing legal principles applicable to the case.

In construing a document, the court is not bound to treat a term of a contract as a condition, merely because it is termed a condition. Whether the term is a primary condition, the breach of which gives rise to a right to terminate the contract, or is of a secondary nature, sometimes termed a 'warranty', though this term is falling out of favour, as is illustrated in *Moschi v Lep Air Services Ltd* [1973] AC 331 (HL), is a matter for the court. Thus, in a contract stating that it was a condition that salesmen should make weekly calls, a failure to make such calls regularly was held not to amount to a breach of a term which the law would treat as a condition, in the sense of entitling the other party to terminate the contract (*Schuler (L) AG v Wickman Machine Tool Sales Ltd* [1974] AC 235 (HL)).

5.06 Principles of construction

In construing a document the primary rule is that the document must be construed as a whole. The effect of this rule is that earlier decisions on the meaning of words are of limited value, since they will inevitably have been contained in a different context. It is for this reason that the cases in Part III contain extracts from the text of the judgments, so that one can better appreciate what motivated the court in determining the construction in each case.

Words will be given their dictionary meaning, and reliance will be placed on the *Oxford English Dictionary* for this purpose. If there is an obvious error, the court will read the document as though the error had been corrected in a way that a reasonable man would have expected it to read (*Adamastos Shipping Co Ltd v Anglo-Saxon Petroleum Co Ltd* [1959] AC 133 (HL)).

The object will be to give effect to the intentions of the parties as ascertained by interpretation, and to avoid any absurdity, or legal ineffectiveness where possible. If necessary the court will supply missing words, discard surplusage and modify or transpose words, so that the document shall play the part intended by the parties (*Federal Steam Navigation Co v Dept of Trade & Industry* [1974] 1 WLR 505 (HL)).

In *Adamastos Shipping Co Ltd v Anglo-Saxon Petroleum Co Ltd* [1959] AC 133 (HL) for example, a clause which referred to 'this bill of lading' was incorporated in a charterparty, whilst the main body of the charterparty contained a clause stating that the provisions of the US statute applied (which provided that the terms should not be applicable to charterparties). There was a further clause which provided that 'It is agreed that the Chamber of Shipping War Risks Clauses, New Jason Clause, Paramount Clause and Both to Blame Collision Clause as attached are to be incorporated in this charterparty'.

To make sense of the contract, the House of Lords held that the phrase 'this bill of lading' contained in a separate slip intended to be attached to shipping documents, should be read as though it said 'this charterparty'; and as to the US statute, they held that the provision stating that it should not apply to charterparties should be ignored as meaningless. In other words, only by considering the document as a whole could the court make sense of it, and the court did not hesitate to discard what would hinder its validity.

5.07 Established rules

In the course of centuries the common law has thrown up a number of principles which it uses in construing documents; these may be summarised as follows:

(1) Recitals and marginal notes

These will be taken into account in so far as they may help to ascertain the meaning and effect of the document. This should be borne in mind when drafting a document, and a statement of the objects of the document, and the results expected by the parties should so far as practicable be included in recitals.

General words are controlled by a recital. In *Re Moon, Ex p Dawes* (1886) 17 QBD 275 a debtor executed a deed of composition which recited that he was possessed of or entitled to the real and personal estate specified in a schedule to the deed. The operative part assigned to the trustee 'all and singular the several properties, chattels, and effects set forth in the schedule hereto, and all the estate, right, title, interest, claim, and demand,' of the debtor 'in, to, and upon the said chattels, properties, and effects, and all other the estate (if any)' of the debtor. Thus in this case the deed was intended only to apply to the property set forth in the schedule.

Lindley LJ at p 288: 'Anyone accustomed to legal documents must be very much struck with the parcels in this deed; I never saw, and I do not suppose anyone else ever saw, such an enumeration. The first part of the description is, "all and singular the several properties, chattels, and effects set forth in the schedule hereto". Of course the words "in the schedule" show pretty clearly what is meant; there is no ambiguity about it. Then comes what is known as the "all the estate" clause, which is intelligible enough to persons accustomed to legal instruments. Then comes something which strikes one as very odd and incomprehensible. Apart from the recitals we should not know what was meant—"and all other the estate (if any) of the said William Moon". It does not say in what, and, if there were no recitals to throw light upon it, I do not know that anyone could make out the meaning of it. . . . If there was nothing to explain these words, I cannot help thinking that the whole thing would be extremely ambiguous. But the ambiguity is removed at once when you look at the recitals.'

Lopes LJ at p 289: 'There are several well-established rules applicable to the construction of deeds. One is this, that, if the operative part of a deed is clear, and the recitals are not clear, the operative part must prevail. Again, if the recitals are clear, but the operative part is ambiguous, the recitals control the operative part. If, again, the operative part and the recitals are both clear, but the one is inconsistent with the other, the operative part must prevail.

Now we are not asked to rectify this deed; we are only asked to construe it, and the question is, whether Dawes, the trustee of the deed, is an assignee of the debtor's life interest under the settlement. It appears to me perfectly plain that the operative part of the deed is ambiguous. If that is so, then, according to the rules of construction to which I have alluded, it becomes necessary to look at the recitals. And the recitals are as clear as they can well be. There is only one possible meaning.'

(2) Expressio unius personae vel rei est exclusio alterius

To avoid inconsistency a specific provision which is expressed in some detail, will necessarily indicate that anything inconsistent with the detailed list or provision will be excluded. It is a warning against the inclusion of great detail unless one is quite clear that it is necessary.

(3) Ejusdem generis

Where specific words are followed by general words eg 'and others', the general words will be treated as limited to the class of the specific words.

(4) Verba chartarum fortius accipiuntur contra proferentem

This is usually referred to as 'the contra proferentem rule'. An ambiguity which can be resolved by construing the document against the interests of the party responsible for the ambiguous provision will be so resolved.

(5) Noscitur a sociis

Words associated with each other will be construed on a common basis.

(6) Words repeated in a document

These will normally be given the same meaning throughout, unless the document as a whole does not allow of the application of this rule of consistency, as in the case of *Watson v Haggitt* [1928] AC 127 (PC).

(7) Whole document or statute to be studied when construing

In *Att-Gen v Ernest Augustus (Prince) of Hanover* [1957] AC 436 the court had to consider the following. By virtue of the statute of 1705 it was enacted that Princess Sophia, Electress of Hanover, and the issue of her body . . . 'should be naturalized'. The question arose whether the Respondent acquired his British nationality immediately before the coming into force of the British Nationality Act 1948 which repealed the Statute of 1705; if so the Respondent would retain his British nationality.

Viscount Simonds at p 463. 'On the one hand, the proposition can be accepted that "it is a settled rule that the preamble cannot be made use of to control the enactments themselves where they are expressed in clear and unambiguous terms". . . . I quote the words of Chitty LJ, which were cordially approved by Lord Davey in *Powell v Kempton Park Racecourse Co Ltd* [1899] AC 143 (CA). On the other hand, it must often be difficult to say that any terms are clear and unambiguous until they have been studied in their context. That is not to say that the warning is to be disregarded against creating or imagining an ambiguity in order to bring in the aid of the preamble. It means only that the elementary rule must be observed that no one should profess to understand any part of a statute or of any other document before he had read the whole of it. Until he has done so he is not entitled to say that it or any part of it is clear and unambiguous. To say, then, that you must not call in aid the preamble in order to create an ambiguity in effect means very little, and, with great respect to those who have from time to time invoked this rule, I would suggest that it is better stated by saying that the context of the preamble is not to influence the meaning otherwise ascribable to the enacting part unless there is a compelling reason for it. And I do not propose to define that expression except negatively by saying (as I have said before) that it is not to be found merely in the fact that the enacting words go further than the preamble has indicated. Still less can the preamble affect the meaning of the enacting words when its own meaning is in doubt.

With these principles, if they can be called principles, in mind, I turn once more to the statute we have to consider and I find, first, that it is only the narrower scope of the objective as stated in the preamble which is relied on to restrict the emphatic generality of the enacting words, and secondly, that it is at least a matter of doubt what is the scope of the preamble itself. For, as I have already indicated, the clumsy phrase "they, in Your Majesty's lifetime . . . should be naturalized" is susceptible of meaning that an Act should be passed in the lifetime of the Queen for the naturalization of her descendants born and unborn. In these circumstances I must reject also the argument of the Attorney-General which is based on the context of the preamble.'

5.08 Time

It is important to state precisely a time when something is to be done, and it is equally important that your client should know how the law would interpret the clause or clauses so providing.

There is an ancient rule that performance due on a particular day allows the person who is to perform up to midnight on that day to make the payment or do the act required (*Startup v MacDonald* (1843) 6 Man & G 593). If the day proves to be a non-business day, then he must perform on the business day prior to the contract date, except in the case of legal proceedings, when he may take the required step on the next day that the courts are open for business; also in the case of bills of exchange under the Bills of Exchange Act 1882 ss 14(1) and 92, the payer is allowed to pay on the next business day.

For a further consideration of time periods see below at 12.01.

5.09 Payment to be punctual or on demand

To require that payment is to be punctual adds nothing to the obligation of the payer (*Maclaine v Gatty* [1921] 1 AC 376 (HL); *Mardorf Peach & Co Ltd v Attica Sea Carriers Corpn of Liberia; The Laconia* [1977] AC 850 (HL)); and to require that payment shall be made on demand does not deprive the payer of a reasonable time to satisfy himself that the person demanding payment is authorised, and, further, to obtain the means of payment (*Dodds v Walker* [1981] 1 WLR 1027 (HL)).

5.10 Arbitration

An alternative means of dealing with disputes by court proceedings is to provide that disputes shall be referred to arbitration. Arbitration, if suggested, will almost always meet with approval by the parties, because at the time of negotiation they are in a friendly mood and do not expect that anything other than a dispassionate question of interpretation is likely to arise.

The question of the governing law will still need to be settled and normally you would adopt the law of the place where the arbitration is to take place. Thus if you decided to arbitrate in Switzerland, you would need to adopt the law of the particular Canton selected, and have the agreement examined and passed by a Swiss lawyer on behalf of your client.

5.11 Compulsory arbitration

Before adopting arbitration as a compulsory means of dealing with disputes, it is important that the parties should be made aware of what is involved. Whilst arbitration has the advantage of privacy, it may prove somwhat more expensive than a court hearing, unless the dispute is a friendly dispute, which is a rare occurrence. It is also likely to be time-consuming. Arbitrators will charge by the hour for the time spent on the matter: one does not pay a judge of the law courts for his time.

If, nevertheless, arbitration is to be provided for, it is highly desirable that it shall be governed by one of the organisations which arrange arbitrations. Such established organisations are The London Court of International Arbitration, 75 Cannon St,

London EC4; The International Chamber of Commerce, 38 Cours Albert 1er, 75008 Paris; The American Arbitration Assoc, 140 West 61st St, New York, NY 10020. They have a set of rules, in place of the Rules of the Supreme Court (applicable to litigation in the law courts), whereby an arbitrator can control the proceedings, by, for example, making orders against a party who neglects to take steps called for from him, such an order binding him to act, on pain of dismissal of his claim or defence.

Even with those powers, it is a noticeable fact that on numerous occasions a party to an arbitration is forced to seek the court's help because one party has failed to take any step in the proceedings for a year or more.

5.12 A friendly arbitration

An alternative, not commonly found, is to provide that arbitration shall apply if at the time when a dispute arises the parties agree to arbitration rather than institute court proceedings. This would include referring the matter to one of the recognised arbitration bodies at a named venue. It is not a legally binding provision. It is a mere agreement to agree, but it does at least give rise to a situation where, if the parties decide or can be persuaded to operate under that clause, and refer the dispute to arbitration, they have an agreed procedure laid down in the agreement, albeit only binding in honour. Proceedings thus initiated ought to be as friendly an arbitration as one could expect, much less costly and disposed of fairly quickly, but in such a case it is a matter of judgment at the time whether either party is likely to prove difficult.

It is a misconception to assume that parties will never follow an agreed clause merely because the lawyers inform them that it is not legally binding. If they do refuse, nothing has been lost. Some are proud to be men of honour but it would be advisable in such a case to provide expressly that the other provisions of the document are accepted as legally binding and enforceable.

Chapter 6

The Sentence and the Paragraph

'Soon the human has a verbal substitute within himself theoretically for every object in the world. Thereafter he carries the world around with him by means of this organisation. And he can manipulate this world in the privacy of his room or when he lies down on his bed in the dark.'

J B Watson, *Behaviourism*

'If others found it incomprehensible how a human soul could invent language, to me it is incomprehensible how a human soul could be what it is and not, by that fact alone—without the help of a mouth and without the presence of a society— be led to invent language.'

J G von Herder, *Essay on the Origin of Language*

6.01 The sentence

There can be found well over two hundred different attempts at a definition of the sentence.

Fries, in his book *The Structure of English* quotes a number of possible definitions including one by Bloomfield which he accepts as a suitable general definition: 'Each sentence is an independent linguistic form, not included by virtue of any grammatical construction in any larger linguistic form'.

It appears advantageous to define the sentence in speech more broadly that the sentence in writing. In speech it may be said to be 'a discrete unit of utterance' separated, where more than one, from other such units by recognisable pauses, whilst a sentence, composed to be written, is a collocation of thoughts syntactically self-contained.

To the question 'When shall I see you again?' the answer 'Tomorrow' is a sentence in speech, a complete unit of utterance. It has implied contents which it is not necessary to utter, such as 'I shall be coming . . .'

Strang defines the sentence generally as 'Those linguistic sequences that have internal but no external grammatical relations—which are grammatical structures, and self-contained ones.' The out-of-date analysis of a sentence as containing a subject and a predicate, the latter including a verb and an object, together sometimes, with an indirect object, can be shown only to apply in the case of model, stereotyped, formal, sentences. As Strang says, it is necessary in English to define a sentence since it is a language in which disjunction of what is grammatically self-contained from what is not, is one of the most fundamental features of language. Sentences are meaningful structures made of other usually, but not necessarily, smaller, meaningful structures.

An utterance, however, is often 'performative' ie an accompaniment to an action as 'I do' in the marriage ceremony accompanied by the giving of a ring. Compare this with 'operative' statements as in a legal document such as: 'the Vendor hereby conveys No 2 Railway Cuttings, Clapham', followed by a signature of the deed.

Today the approach is not normative but perceptive of usage at all levels; not legislative but descriptive, testing what is seen and heard by its effectiveness.

The parsing of sentences into parts of speech, of which there are, according to some, eight, to others, ten, serves little or no purpose towards accomplishment in composition, and is in any event, limited to those same formally, and teleologically, constructed sentences. C T Onions takes a more orthodox approach to the analysis of sentences in *An Advanced English Syntax*.

Good composition is intuitive requiring familiarity with the language and its literature. The test is whether it reads well and conveys meaning, without the need for (allowing for the nature of the subject matter) undue concentration on the part of the reader.

To define a sentence scientifically presents problems, and it would be out of place in this work to go into the matter at length. What may be regarded as an attempt at a scientific definition is that of Fries in *The Structure of English*: 'Speech acts that are language always consist of lexical items in some kind of structure.'

In legal documents sentences will, naturally, be formal, and the same rule applies to all legal work, except perhaps in recording statements of witnesses.

6.02 Manipulating words

It is not possible to write without thinking. The greater the effort of concentration you put into the task of mentally constructing the sentences you intend to use, before you start to write, the better chance there is of saying what you mean. You must of course first decide what it is that you mean to say, and ensure that when you have composed the substance of the material, it does in fact say what you mean as clearly as you can put it. It does require effort and some patience together with a willingness to revise carefully, and, if it appears advantageous, continually, until no further advantage can be obtained by further changes.

It is a good rule not to start to write until you have assembled in your mind as clear a notion as possible of the matter which you are about to set down.

6.03 Features of sentences relating to law

Because the law operates upon or in relation to persons, the subject of sentences in legal documents will usually be legal persons ie real persons or juristic persons (companies and other recognised bodies or groups which are treated as one). Generally, one should avoid sentences where the subject is an inanimate object eg to take a somewhat basic example, 'The property shall be maintained in good order'. This example may imply an ellipsis by the omission of a reference to the parties, but in putting them in, it is not satisfactory to use the passive case, by for example adding to the previous sentence 'by the lessee'. Use the active voice instead, and show the relationship of each party to the matter in hand eg 'The lessee shall maintain the property in good order to the reasonable satisfaction of the lessor'.

6.04 The sentence and the paragraph

The essential rule is never to pass a sentence into use that is longer than is essential, and never to write a paragraph that deals with more than one idea, concept or feature of the draft. In a legal document a paragraph may consist of a single sentence, a feature probably more often adopted than not.

Make sure you understand the sentence you have written and that it says what you want to say, before leaving it as first drafted.

An equally important rule is, that having satisfied yourself that your choice of words has been well made, you should consider whether the structure of the sentence can be improved from the syntactical point of view. See whether a rearrangement of the words chosen will improve the impact of the sentence and make its meaning stand out more clearly. If so, make the necessary changes.

6.05 Use of subparagraphs within the paragraph

On occasion you will need to construct a sentence or a paragraph that deals with more than one facet, in which case you should consider breaking up the sentence or paragraph into a main statement followed by subclauses suitably numbered. The construction will then have more than one predicate, thus:

> (1) Main concept, or first statement (normally subject and verb):
>> (*a*) first predicate; or
>> (*b*) second predicate.

Think of the main concept and make sure that each predicate can be joined to it, so that one has a complete sentence whichever predicate is attached to the subject and verb, or other first statement. The main concept cannot be joined to both at the same time.

Alternately, the phrases to be separated out may be cumulative (conjunctive) rather than disjunctive in which case the pattern will be:

> (1) Main concept, or first statement (normally subject and verb):

(*a*) first modifying phrase, and

(*b*) second modifier, and . . .

So that in this case, the main concept can be joined to several cumulative phrases at once.

In general, sentences and paragraphs dealing with matters of law are much shorter than those used by novelists, essayists and other literary men. The reason for this lies in the difference in the subject matter, since the rules are substantially the same, though the need to comply with them falls more heavily on the lawyer than on the novelist.

A glance at the works of Carlyle, Kipling, Conan Doyle, Flaubert, Tolstoy and other such writers shows the use of paragraphs of some length, since writers in that genre are describing, in detail, scenes, emotions, aspirations and the like, and these matters are not to be properly expressed in a few terse sentences. And if one looks at essayists, or historians, Macaulay or Burke for example, the paragraphs are even longer. In *Nature and Industrialisation*, Alasdair Clayre has gathered together passages from writers in all walks of life—poets, novelists, political commentators, artists, musicians, travellers, philosophers and others—showing a variety of styles, but on the whole (leaving aside poets) a common principle.

6.06 Selection of synonyms

In para 1.11 we dealt with semantics, the science of the choice of the most appropriate word to convey the meaning intended, a vital step in composition. Here, we discuss the selection of alternative synonyms.

Fowler, in his *Modern English Usage*, recommended a list of preferences in constructing a piece of writing. These were that one should prefer:

the familiar word to the far-fetched

the concrete expression to the abstract

the single word to the circumlocution

the short word to the long

the Saxon word to the Romance

The last two are open to criticism, in that you should choose the right word whatever its length and only if there is a choice which does not affect the meaning to be conveyed, should you make that distinction; and as to the preference for Saxon over Romance, that seems to be nothing but a prejudice which so often cannot be exercised, even if it should, for want of the knowledge whether a preferred word has its origins in the one language or the other.

In Chapter 1, attention is called to the existence of the aura of uncertainty which surrounds all words. It is a feature which may be reduced by the context in which the word appears. That aura is naturally greater in the case of abstract words as compared with the concrete word, hence the preference for the concrete over the abstract. It is a matter to keep in mind, since it has been observed that the vagueness of the abstract expression will be preferred by a mind that is temporarily lazy.

6.07 Verbiage

The admonition to avoid unnecessary words and keep your material as short as possible is often heard. It is a question of balancing the written matter against the object to be achieved. What tends to produce unnecessary words is a desire to emphasise some point, whereupon there is the temptation to pepper your sentences with excess adjectives and adverbs to achieve the emphasis, with the result that sometimes the same nuance is given twice eg 'must necessarily', if it must be done it is necessary that it be done. This fault, to endeavour to create a special effect, can be self-defeating, and for that reason the admonition is sound.

The expression 'as to' is just another example of what usually turns out to be unnecessary verbiage. It also happens to be the subject of one of the extracts in Part III, which failed to operate as a disjunctive term as intended. It is just one example of vague catch-phrases which are best avoided. Most such phrases, we may safely guess, have been adopted in desperation after failing to find the appropriate conjunction.

An expression such as: 'So far as X is concerned the Act does not apply in this case' is verbiage for 'The Act does not apply to the case against X'. The words 'So far as X is concerned' are verbiage for a reference to X, and the words 'in his case' represent further verbiage made necessary to connect X with the opening (unnecessary) phrase.

6.08 Mixed metaphors

The danger of mixing metaphors is well known, but not so readily avoided unless one is vigilant. It remains something to be on the look-out for. In technical or legal compositions metaphors should only be adopted as a last resort.

Some overworked or misused metaphors are listed by Fraser in *The Complete Plain Words* and discussed fairly fully. A sample of the contents is:

Background	Blueprint	Bottleneck
Breakdown	Catalyst	Ceiling
Interface	Parameter	Syndrome
Target		

Chapter 7

Modifying and Assembling; Syntactical Ambiguities

Polonius: 'What do you read my Lord?'
Hamlet: 'Words, Words, Words.'

Shakespeare, Hamlet

'He that thinks with more extent than another will want
words of larger meaning.'

Dr Samuel Johnson, in Boswell's Life of Johnson

7.01 Multiple modifiers

A modifier is a word or group of words that adds to the meaning
of another word.

Great care is needed when assigning to a noun or noun phrase
a number of adjectives, adverbs or other modifying words in a
sentence. Ensure that they do in fact effectively modify the
'magnet' word or phrase to which they are intended to be
attached or with which they are intended to be associated.

In a case of which an extract is given in Part III, for example,
it was determined that a gift to any 'religious philanthropic
or charitable institution' leaves open the question whether the
charitable 'institution' must also be religious.

7.02 Oblique modifiers

Ambiguity can also be caused where there are two nouns or
phrases, and the modifiers are so placed syntactically that it is
not clear whether they all apply to each noun or phrase, or
whether one or some apply only to one noun or phrase. Thus
suppose that an agreement includes the following provision:

> Should the grantee fail to render a true account of the
> royalties due including royalties due from the sublicensee,

the licensor shall have the right to call upon the grantee
forthwith and without notice to terminate the sublicence.

This does not make clear whether the licensor need not give
the grantee notice when requiring that the grantee is to terminate the sublicence, or whether the grantee may terminate the
sublicence without the grantee giving notice to the sublicensee.

7.03 Inapt modifiers

The use of the adverb 'substantially' is common. It is a useful
word, and on the whole unobjectionable. It suggests that the
person who has the benefit of the covenant is not going to be
too hard on the one obliged to perform it, if he has not acted
with precision, for example where the obligation is satisfied
'where performance has been substantially in accordance with
the contract'. But to say that one would be satisfied where
performance is 'substantially complete' poses a problem, either
performance is complete or not, and the modifier becomes virtually meaningless. Contrast this with the familiar modifier used
by lawyers, namely, the term 'reasonable', but note that this
word, being derived from 'reason', does not present such a
problem, since the law is used to considering reasons for actions
or for failing to act.

7.04 Syntactical ambiguity in collocations

(1) False nexus with nouns
A provision in the terms: 'A patentee granting a licence in the
United Kingdom must register the licence in the Patent Office
without delay' leaves open the question which is to be in the
UK, the patentee or the licence granted? If should read: 'Any
patent licence granted in the United Kingdom by the patentee
must be registered without delay.'

(2) False nexus with verbs
In an agreement, the following term exhibits an ambiguity: 'The
seller agrees to replace goods found to be defective provided
that they have not been tampered with within twenty-eight
days'. The verbs 'found', 'replace' and 'tampered with' are in

an ambiguous relationship, leaving unclear the question whether the twenty-eight days relates to the verbal phrase 'found to be defective' or the verbal phrase 'tampered with'. The clause should read: 'The seller agrees that if the goods are found, within twenty-eight days of purchase, to be defective and have not been tampered with, he will replace them.'

(3) Prepositional nexus confusions

What exactly is the restricted siting of a billboard in the following statement: 'licensee may not without licensor's consent erect any advertisement hoarding on any building higher than ten metres'. Is the restriction applicable to the greatest height of the advertisement, or the height of the building?

7.05 Pronouns and their equivalents

The following careless construction is literally ambiguous though it is not likely to be misunderstood, nevertheless such constructions are to be avoided. 'Where a licensee has received an enquiry from a potential purchaser in the excluded territory he shall refer the matter to the licensor'. The pronoun 'he' could apply either to the licensee or the potential purchaser. In other words, pronouns or pronominal phrases should be regarded as danger signals, and readily discarded in favour of the noun if there is any risk of ambiguity.

7.06 Conjunctions: 'and' and 'or'

Words operating as conjunctions or verbal auxiliaries are a constant source of problems in construing documents. For a comprehensive view, one of the larger judicial dictionaries should be consulted. The following is a representative sample:

(1) And/or

This much maligned combination has its uses, and in any event, is so popular that it will constantly recur whatever may be written in derogation of its use. The point to bear in mind is to consider the possible combinations that it postulates. As an example, take the following case: 'I hear that you have suggested some amendments and/or additions to my draft on which

I cannot comment as I have not yet seen them.' This presupposes that:

(*a*) there may be some amendments only;
(*b*) there may be some additions only;
(*c*) there may be both amendments and additions.

The 'and/or' in this case is not objectionable.

If, however, A says to B 'You may have a licence for the product and/or the process', the '/or' is superfluous since the choice rests with the person addressed who may take either or both.

In a bequest by will to 'Margaret and/or John', who were husband and wife, Farwell J held that the gift should be construed as a joint gift to both, or to the survivor if one were to predecease the testator (*Re Lewis, Goronwy v Richards* [1942] 2 All ER 364).

(2) 'and' intended to apply to either or both

Where 'and' is used rather than 'and/or' for this purpose, the question arises whether 'and' may be read as 'or'.

Attempts have been made in some disputes involving the conjunction 'and', to show that it ought to be read disjunctively as though it were equivalent to 'or'. This was done in the case of *Adams v Richardson and Starling Ltd* [1969] 1 WLR 1645 (CA) an extract of which is given in Part III, where a form of guarantee was followed by a clause setting out the customer's right to have the work re-done if found faulty. The latter part of the clause was in effect an attempt to cut down the width of the guarantee, so as to restrict it to re-doing the treatment on the original area, whereas what had happened was that the failure properly to treat the premises led to a spreading of the trouble to other areas. It was held that the two parts of the clause were one whole, rejecting the attempt to read 'and' as 'or'.

(3) 'and' as an alternative

Another type of case which leads to ambiguity is the use of 'and' for alternatives eg: 'In the event of a default by the licensee, the licensor and his successors in title may terminate this agreement and retake possession of the machinery.' Here the 'and' after licensor should be 'or'. Alternatively the phrase

'Licensor and his successors in title as the case my be' could be used.

A good example of 'and' read as meaning 'or' is contained in *Re Eades* (1920) 2 Ch 353 where a testator directed that the trustees of his will should out of specified funds pay ten per cent to such 'religious, charitable and philanthropic' objects as certain persons should appoint.

Held: 'And' must be read as 'or'; whereupon, as one or more of the selected objects might be merely philanthropic and not necessarily charitable, no general charitable intent was shown, so that the gift in favour of charity failed.

Sargant J at p 356: 'Now it is plainly inadmissible to read the words as requiring one only of these two further characteristics. But is this gift confined by the language of the will to objects that are necessarily charitable in the technical sense of that term? The word "philanthropic" by itself is undoubtedly too wide, and to render the gift good one must hold that every object of the gift should, in addition to the qualification of being "philanthropic" have the further qualification of being either "religious" or "charitable" or both. Now it is plainly inadmissible to read the words as requiring one only of these two further characteristics, that is as denoting objects which, in addition to being philanthropic, are also either religious or charitable. And the only possible constructions are therefore two, the first being one on which all the objects are to be both religious and charitable and philanthropic; and the second being one on which religious objects, and charitable objects and philanthropic objects are within the area of selection—but it is not necessary that any single object should have more than one of these three characteristics.

Such a construction as the second is sometimes referred to as disjunctive construction, and as involving a change of the word "and" into "or". This is a short and compendious way of expressing the result of the construction but I doubt whether it indicates accurately the mental conception by which the result is reached. That conception is one I think which regards the word "and" as used conjunctively and by way of addition, for the purpose of enlarging the number of objects within the area of selection; and it does not appear to be a false mental conception, or one really at variance with the ordinary use of language, merely because it involves in the result that the qualifications for selection are alternate or disjunctive.

Further, the greater the number of the qualifications or characteristics enumerated, the more probable, as it seems to me, is a construction which regards them as multiplying the kinds of classes of objects within the area of selection, rather than multiplying the number of qualifications to be complied with, and so diminishing the objects within the area of selection. In the present case the ordinary careful student of the English language and literature, would, I think, almost certainly come to the conclusion that the three epithets here are epithets creating conjunctive or cumulative classes of objects, not epithets creating conjunctive or cumulative qualifications for each object . . . I decide that the gift is not necessarily charitable and is therefore void for uncertainty.'

A further example of disputes arising from the use of conjunctives is whether 'or without' is to be read as 'and without'. This was the question in *Brown (RF) & Co Ltd v Harrison, Hourani v Same* (1927) 137 LT 549 (CA). Without the fault or privity of the defendants, and in spite of the vigilance of the ship's officers, the plaintiff's good were stolen from the defendants' steamer at Liverpool by the stevedores' men. The men were engaged by the ship's agents to discharge the cargo at Vera Cruz where the ship called before going to Tampico. There was an action for non-delivery.

The defendants appealed from McKinnon J's decision that they had not shown that they were excused by the provisions of the Carriage of Goods by Sea Act 1924; and that in those provisions the word 'or' must be read as 'and' conjunctively where it occurs in rule 2(q) of art IV.

By Art IV, r 2, of the Schedule to the Carriage of Goods by Sea Act 1924, 'Neither the carrier nor the ship shall be responsible for loss or damage arising or resulting from—(a) Act, neglect, or default of the master, mariner, pilot, or the servants of the carrier in the navigation or in the management of the ship . . . (q) Any other cause arising without the actual fault or privity of the carrier, or without the fault or neglect of the agents or servants of the carrier, but the burden of proof shall be on the person claiming the benefit of this exception to show that neither the actual fault of privity of the carrier nor the fault or neglect of the agents or servants of the carrier contributed to the loss or damage.'

Bankes LJ at p 552: 'In construing these articles which form part of the statute . . . one must begin by realising that here the Legislature have imposed this distinct statutory obligation in reference to the goods which the carrier undertakes to carry. The statute then proceeds to set up what under former practice would have been the exceptions agreed upon between the parties, and those are the exceptions cutting down that statutory obligation which is imposed by s 2 of art III . . . and the first question raised which the learned judge had to decide, and which we have to decide, is, what is included in those words "management of the ship". Can it be said that the act of these stevedores' servants, in raiding the cargo and stealing these goods, within the meaning of this subsection is an act which occurred in the management of the ship? MacKinnon J has said that it cannot, and I agree with him . . . Speaking first of all in reference to the language of the statute itself, I think that, as an ordinary rule of construction of this language, when you find in the first place the Legislature imposing this particular statutory duty upon the shipowner in reference, amongst other things, to the discharge of the goods carried, and then, when it comes to enumerate the exceptions it has no exception dealing specifically with the goods, but it has an exception dealing with the ship and the management of the ship as it may affect the goods, in order to bring any particular matter within the exception it must be something which can be said to be in the management of the ship. Therefore I should say, apart altogether from authority, that if all the shipowner can prove is an act which has relation to the goods, and the goods alone, and has no relation to the ship itself, it is an act which is a well recognised act in relation to a ship, it is true, but it is a separate and an independent act and independent of the ship . . .' at p554: 'Reference has been made to a decision in the Supreme Court of the United States in which Holmes J delivered the opinion of the court, and I think it is satisfactory to find that the law as interpreted in this country so exactly corresponds with the view of the law as expressed by Holmes J in reference to the Harter Act in this American decision . . . So far as the burden of proof is concerned, and the latter portion of the clause, it is plain that the obligation is laid upon the person seeking the benefit of the exception to establish not only that the loss has been without his actual fault or privity, but also that it has been without the fault or neglect of his agents or servants; and that, one would think, is reasonable and natural, because really to contend that the statute has conferred an exception from liability upon a carrier who deliberately incites a man to steal the goods and then claims exemption from his act because his servants or agents had been guilty of no fault or neglect, is to impose an obligation upon the court which it would be extremely loth to accept unless it was absolutely compelled to do so. Now Mr Clement Davies says that the court must put that construction upon the statute because of the opening words which define the exception and which, as he says, draw a distinction between the act of the carrier and the act of his servant, and that it is sufficient to bring himself within the exception if he proves either that the loss was without his actual fault or privity or that it was without the fault or neglect of his agents or servants, and he lays the whole stress of his arguments upon the fact that the clause is drafted in this form, "Any other cause arising without the actual fault or privity of the carrier, or without the fault or neglect of the agents or servants," and he says that the word "or" is there read disjunctively, and that you cannot read it otherwise, except by assuming that the draftsman has made a mistake or that it is competent for the court to alter "or" into "and". But with great respect, it is doing no injustice either to the draftsman or the language, to use the word "or" conjunctively and not disjunctively. There is abundant authority for doing that. It seems to me that it is quite imperative upon the court to do it in this case, first, because it is only by doing it that you can bring the two branches of the subsection into agreement, and, secondly, that unless you do it you adopt a construction of the exception which it seems to me inconceivable that the Legislature should ever have contemplated for a moment. I think therefore that that point fails.'

(4) 'and' intended where 'or' is more appropriate

A clause providing that the licensee 'shall not use the patent for any purpose other than for products to be supplied to haber-dashers and outfitters' would be better if the 'and' were 'or'.

(5) Inclusive 'and'

This is the normal case where the 'and' is intended to act as a simple conjunction requiring that both conditions be satisfied, or where each of two parties shall be treated as one.

In *Re Best, Jarvis v Birmingham Corpn* [1904] 2 Ch 354 a testator left a gift for 'such charitable and benevolent institutions' as the trustees in their discretion should determine. Had there not been earlier cases where a similar bequest had failed, the matter would hardly have been arguable. Farwell J in giving judgment said: 'Having regard to the curiously technical meaning which has been given by the English courts to the word "charitable" I am not surprised that the testator should have desired that the institutions should be not only charitable but should be also benevolent . . . and I see no reason for reading the conjunction "and" as "or" '.

(6) Exclusive 'or'

'Any employee who, in any month, has lost no time off duty or has achieved an increase of at least five per cent in his output will be entitled to a bonus calculated on his average weekly pay.' These two alternatives of no loss of time and increase in output, will each give the entitlement, but what if both are achieved? This would in any event appear to be necessary for the second condition to be satisfied ie the first is surely contained in the second more often than not? Clearly that type of drafting arises only from careless thinking.

(7) Inclusive 'or': whether 'or' may be read as 'and'

There have also been cases where 'or' has presented a problem because the provision in which it occurred seemed to call for 'and'. In *Federal Steam Navigation Co v Dept of Trade and Industry* [1974] 1 WLR 505 (HL) the question arose whether proceedings could be brought against the owner, or the captain, of a ship which had discharged oil in forbidden waters, or against both of them. The House of Lords held that 'in logic there is no rule that "or" shall carry an exclusive force', and they held that proceedings could be brought against either or both.

The same situation occurs in the following sentence: 'Any employee who is required to be re-deployed in another of the company's works will be paid his moving expenses or his costs of travel.' The intention would be to pay both if both are incurred.

(8) Exegetic 'or'

The expression 'horse or quadruped' uses 'or' by way of explanation, to make clear that what is wanted is a four-footed draft animal.

7.07 Disjunctives

Much of this chapter has been devoted to consideration of 'and' as a conjunction and we need now to consider whether 'and' can be treated as disjunctive. In *Adams v Richardson and Starling Ltd* [1969] 1 WLR 1645 (CA) the defendants were requested to treat the dry rot in a town house, the owner of which wanted a thorough treatment. The defendant offered a guarantee in these terms:

> Adequate treatment to accessible timbers carried out by our own trained operatives is covered by our written ten year guarantee . . . Richardson and Starling Ltd guarantee the efficacy of the treatment they apply to timber or masonry for the eradication of insect or fungal attack . . . and subject to the undernoted exclusions, will re-treat free of charge any such timber or masonry showing signs of reinfestation during the period of ten years from the date of treatment. This guarantee holds good to any owner for the time being of the property described, during the period of the guarantee.

Some five years after the work was done the premises were found to be reinfested and the damage had spread to other areas which had not been treated.

The defendants argued that the guarantee was qualified by the second part commencing with the words 'and subject to . . . will re-treat free of charge' so that their obligation was only to re-treat the areas previously done.

By a majority, the court held that the guarantee was all one document so that the second part of the guarantee could not be separated from the first by reading 'and' as effectively a disjunctive; Lord Denning dissenting.

Salmon L J at p 1652: 'One possible view is that the operative part of the guarantee—namely the paragraph starting with the words "Richardson and Starling Ltd" and ending with the word "treatment"—is divided into two separate compartments separated by the word "and". The first compartment contains an absolute warranty . . . that the treatment applied by the specialists to the timber and masonry shall so effectively eradicate dry rot that it will not reappear for ten years. . . . If this is the correct view then the specialists are liable under the first compartment of the guarantee for all the damage caused by any breach of this warranty, promise or undertaking. On this basis I do not think that the second compartment of the guarantee could be effective to cut down the specialists' liability for a breach of their obligations under the first compartment. Had the second compartment been intended to limit the scope of the specialists' liability under the first compartment, the second compartment could hardly have been introduced by a more inept word than the word "and". It is true that on this view the words in the second compartment of the guarantee would be otiose, for they would give the customer little if anything more than that to which he would be entitled for breach of the obligation contained in the first compartment. Damage caused by reinfestation (if recoverable under the first compartment) would surely include the cost of re-treatment referred to in the second compartment. . . . I cannot however persuade myself that the operative part of the guarantee consists of two separate compartments. It seems to me that the guarantee is in reality a single entity and must be read as a whole. Looked at in this way the guarantee is no more than a promise that if any of the timber or masonry treated by the specialists becomes reinfested within ten years from the date of treatment, the specialists will re-treat it free of charge.

This point of construction is by no means easy and I confess that my mind has wavered during the course of the argument. I have, however, finally been turned by the words "Exclusions from the foregoing guarantee. This guarantee does not cover the cost of opening up or of reinstatement nor does it apply to . . ." and then five instances are cited. I cannot accept the argument that these words apply only to the second half of the guarantee, for they are described in the document as "Exclusions from the foregoing guarantee". That must mean the whole guarantee . . . I think that the words "subject to the undernoted exclusions" were quite unnecessary in the second half of the guarantee.'

7.08 The words 'as to' not operating as a disjunctive

In *Gordon v Gordon* (1871) LR 5 HL 254 (HL) it was decided that in a lengthy passage, the current use of 'as to' does not by itself operate to separate the sentences that follow each such use, into independent dispositions of the properties described.

Lord Westbury at p 276: 'The basis of the argument on the part of the appellant was this: that each disposition of the estate in the will became a separate disposition by virtue of the introductory clause of the sentence "as to". Those words are found at the commencement of each sentence. It was argued, therefore, that those introductory words made the several sentences which follow, separate dispositions of the subject matter to which the introductory words referred. . . . My Lords so far as punctuation is concerned, I believe there is no trace of any punctuation in the original will; but whether that be so or not, I entirely concur in the opinion expressed by Sir William Grant in a case before him (*Sanford v Raikes* (1816) 1 Mer 646) that "it is from the words, and from the context, and not from the punctuation" that the meaning of the testator is to be collected. But I entirely deny that those introductory words have the effect of disjoining the two devises.'

7.09 Auxiliaries 'shall' and 'may'

The word 'shall' may be used as an imperative so as to require some specified or ascertainable mode of action, or it may be used modally to indicate an already intended future action. 'May' on the other hand, normally indicates permission, or the existence or provision of a facility to act in a particular way.

Nonetheless, these words have given much trouble when used in documents and statutes. An alternative which occurs in the New Zealand Transport Act 1962, is the phrase 'may require' which has not been interpreted very consistently as appears in the extract from *Parker v Ministry of Transport* (1982) 1 NZLR 209 (CA Wellington) set out in Part III.

The approach to construing 'shall' in a statute or document was well put by a Connecticut court in *State ex rel Donald Barnard v John Ambrogio et al* 162 Conn 491 (1972), not by reference to whether 'shall' or 'may' is used, but by reference to the mode of action for a particular accomplishment:

> In determining whether the provisions of a statute are mandatory or imperative, or merely directory, 'the test most satisfactory and conclusive is, whether the prescribed mode of action is of the essence of the thing to be accomplished, or in other words, whether it relates to matter material or immaterial—to matter of convenience or substance' . . . In the determination . . . as to whether or not a provision . . . is of the essence of the thing to be accomplished . . . significance is to be attached to the nature of the act, . . . [and] the language and form in which the provision is couched.

In that case, the court concluded in the following manner:

> In applying these principles we are satisfied that the provisions are mandatory. Section 7–412 states that the Commission 'shall' not 'may' perform certain obligations. Mandatory, as distinguished from permissive language is used . . . the Commission is called on to act without exercising its own judgment . . . what is required to be done is of substance . . . and not for mere convenience.

7.10 Discretionary 'shall'

Under the New Zealand Broadcasting Act 1976, certain duties are placed upon the Broadcasting Organisation, by virtue of which they 'shall' take into consideration a number of matters applicable to broadcasting. However, the statutory provisions are followed by a discretionary clause, referred to as a privative clause, which provides that their decisions 'shall not' be subject to review. In proceedings by way of certiorari to challenge a decision not to screen 'Death of a Princess' without viewing it, it was held that the authority's decision could not be challenged in the light of the statute (*Hutchins v Broadcasting Corpn of New Zealand* (1981) 2 NZLR 593 (HC Wellington)).

7.11 Need to supply prepositions

The necessity of supplying prepositions arose in a dispute over the meaning of 'between' and of 'divide'. In *Re Dale, Mayer v Wood* [1931] 1 Ch 357 the testator gave all his residuary real estate and personal estate to his trustees upon trust . . . to his wife for life and after her death upon trusts for sale and to divide the proceeds into two equal portions, one to be paid to his son A and the other on trusts for his daughter B and her children.

By codicil he devised his freehold house on trust for his wife for life and on her death for EB for life. He directed his trustees to sell the house and 'divide the proceeds equally between the children of "my son A and my daughter B" '.

A was married with one child, a son; B was married and had six children. A's son having died, the personal representatives of A's son were a defendant. One of B's children, a son, also died and his personal representative was a defendant.

Held: The gift in the codicil included all the testator's grandchildren, both A's and his daughter B's children, so the proceeds were divisible into seven parts.

Luxmoore J at p 363: 'Mr Galbraith admits that in the case of a gift to the children of A and B there is, in any event ambiguity, because on a strict grammatical construction of the phrase it is necessary to supply some word. He says strictly you must supply before the name B either the preposition "of" or the preposition "to," and that that case differs entirely from the present where there is no gift apart from the direction to divide. In such a case he says there is no need to supply any such word, because the phrase, if read literally, is strictly and grammatically complete. . . . In my judgment the result of the authorities seems to be that in the absence of any context or surrounding circumstances a gift to the children of A and B in equal shares, or to be equally divided between the children of A and B, should be construed as a gift in equal shares to the individual B and the children of A. . . . I think it is fair to say that either phrase may be ambiguous and that the ambiguity which necessarily arises from the context or surrounding circumstances is to be solved by that context or by those circumstances.'

7.12 Meaning of 'between'

This word created further problems in *Re Cossentine, Philp v Wesleyan Methodist Local Preachers' Mutual Aid Association Trustees* [1933] Ch 119. The deceased's will provided as follows: 'the rest of my property of whatsoever kind I give to my wife and after her decease to be divided between the Local Preachers' Mutual Aid Society and the heirs of my brother and sisters.'

At the date of the will testator had two sisters living, each of whom had one child, also then living. He had had no sister who had predeceased him. He had no brother then living, but had had one brother who had predeceased him leaving a wife and one child both alive at the date of the will. The testator's wife predeceased him.

Held: That the gift 'to the heirs of my brother and sisters' was a gift to the sisters and the daughter of the deceased brother; and that the gift for division between the charity and the three other donees was a gift in four equal shares.

Maugham J at p 122: 'The will has the merit of great brevity but its true construction is a matter of considerable difficulty. What is the meaning of a gift of personal estate which is "to be divided between the Local Preachers Mutual Aid Society and the heirs of my brother and sisters"? On those words several ambiguities arise. Is the division to be between the charity on the one hand and the heirs of the brother and sisters on the other, or is it to be between all the beneficiaries per capita? Next, do the words "between . . . the heirs of my brother and sisters" mean between the sisters and the heirs of the brother? A further question may arise, what does the word "heirs" mean when used by a testator in regard to the personal estate of living sisters of the testator. . . . I think that . . . dealing with the gift "to the heirs of my brother and sisters" . . . I ought to hold that it is to be construed as being a gift "to my sisters and the heirs of my brother," and not as being a gift "to the heirs of my brother, and the heirs of my sisters."

The remaining question is, how must the division between the charity, the testator's sisters and the deceased brother's heir be made? . . . The history of the word "between" goes back, as does the history of many words in common use, to remote antiquity. Referring to *The Oxford Dictionary* Vol i p 834 shows that if you go as far back as Anglo-Saxon times, the word "between" was etymologically a reference to "two". But there is also in *The Oxford Dictionary* Vol i p 835, para v 19 the statement that "in all senses *between* has been from its earliest appearance, extended to more than two. In Old and Middle English it was so extended in sense 1" (ie the sense of simple position) "in which *among* is now considered better. It is still the only word available to express the relation of a thing to many surrounding things severally and individually, among expressing a relation to them collectively and vaguely." The illustrations given show that in the opinion of the editor it is not in strictness, right to direct a sum to be divided "among A, B and C" but that the correct phrase is, and for many years has been, "between A, B & C".

On the whole I am of the opinion that the gift in the present case "to be divided between the Local Preachers" Mutual Aid Society and the heirs of my brother and sisters" is, according to the natural meaning of the words a gift to be divided between (for in this case I decline to use the word "among") the charity, the sisters, who were alive at the date of the testator's death, and the daughter of his deceased brother—a gift in equal fourth parts,'

Chapter 8

Punctuation and Capitals

'In nature, multitudinous as her forms are, there are only
two fundamentally generic types, corresponding to the two
sense media, space and time. Form, or shape is the natural
expression of space; sound is the natural and direct
expression of time. On the passive side the eye is the receiving organ of space, the ear of the expressions of time.'

R A Wilson, *The Miraculous Birth of Language*

'We begin our interchange with the world with our minds
in a certain genetically determined state, and through inter-
action with an environment, with experience, this state
changes until it reaches a fairly steady mature state, in which
we possess what we call knowledge of language.'

Noam Chomsky, *Men of Ideas*

8.01 Articulateness

The question whether animals and birds have a language is one
of definition: what do we mean by language? The unique feature
of human language is its articulateness, without which it would
do no more than offer a means of vaguely expressing emotional
conditions. That, it seems, is all that most animal and birds can
do. They have no sense of space and time.

Human language achieves articulateness by its discrete form
and by the use of punctuation and other means of breaking up
the sounds into distinct groups or collections of groups, and
into sentences.

8.02 Absence of rules

It is consistent with the fluid nature of the English language
that there should be no firm rules governing the use of punctu-

ation. There is one exception to that, if it really qualifies as an exception and that is the rule that every sentence begins with a capital letter and ends with a full stop. The reason for this fluidity is that punctuation, in common with the composition of English, is more of an art than a science. The draftsman should always bear in mind that punctuation should not be relied upon to correct defective sentence construction. It can be used to help clarify the meaning of a sentence.

The following paragraphs contain what can only be regarded as guidelines to the correct use of punctuation. Fowler in his *Modern English Usage* gives examples of its incorrect use under the heading 'stops'.

8.03 Semicolons

These may be used as follows:

(1) *To make a more cohesive statement* rather than employ two separate short sentences; or to connect main clauses together in what would or could otherwise be two complete sentences, and to avoid the use of an otherwise unmanageable single or unduly long sentence, for example:

> Thus, under subsection (2) it is provided that the supply of means for putting an invention into effect is not an infringement unless the supplier knows, or it is obvious in the circumstances, that those means are intended to be used to put the invention into effect; whilst under subsection (3), which deals with the supply of a staple product, where it is understandably more difficult to prove infringement, it is necessary to establish that the supply was made by the supplier to induce an act of infringement.

> The Act was passed for the protection of a particular class of individuals, dramatic and musical performers; even the short title said so.

> On the other hand the House of Lords has put it rather differently and one finds statements in the speeches to the effect that severance is largely a matter of assisting parties who, whilst exceeding reasonable limits, have done so only trivially or technically; and of not assisting a party who has deliberately tried to impose unduly restrictive terms on another.

(2) *To join a number of predicates to a single subject-cum-verb in a 'formal' sentence.* In this case, the predicates are best listed vertically. This form is seen regularly in statutes.

8.04 Colons

The colon is used to separate two phrases or sentences thereby combining them into one sentence with a suitable pause; in particular it is used to separate a conclusion from the premiss. Where the conclusion is itself a complete sentence it may commence with a capital letter. It may also be used to introduce a list, or to separate two halves of a complete thought. Examples of its various uses follow:

(1) To combine two phrases into a single sentence

So there are these two things about language: it is a purposive undertaking and yet it is carried out with items which are governed by conventional and alterable rules.

(2) To introduce a list

Constitutional law creates obligations just as does the common law (of which it is part), but it reacts against those possessed of political power extra-legally: revolutions, active or passive resistance, the pressures of public opinion; the threat of consequences from these is its sanction.

(3) To separate two balancing halves

Such agreements are not unlawful if the parties choose to abide by them: they are only unenforceable if a party chooses not to abide by them.

(4) To separate the conclusion from the premiss

In business there is something more than barter, exchange, price, payment: there is a sacred faith of man in man.

8.05 Commas

It is not uncommon to read statements to the effect that in legal documents commas are dangerous. Roger Casement is said to have been 'hanged by a comma' (see para 8.06 below), although there were in fact a pair of commas in the statute. A further example of the effect of a comma is contained in *IRC v Hinchy* [1960] AC 748. The respondent made a return for income tax in which he understated the interest received from his Savings Bank account, showing £18 instead of £51 5s 9d. The tax on the amount understated (£33 5s 9d) was £14 5s. The total amount of tax that the respondent should have paid would have been £139 11s 6d. The IRC claimed as a penalty £438 13s 6d calculated as treble the amount of tax payable for the year.

In the earlier Act of 1799 as printed by the Queen's Printer, there is a comma after £20 in the passage 'shall forfeit any sum not exceeding twenty pounds, and treble the duty'. It was argued that that comma showed that 'not exceeding' only governed the £20 and did not apply to 'and treble the duty' so that the General Commissioners had power to reduce the £20 but no power to reduce that part of the penalty which consisted of treble duty.

Lord Reid at p 765: 'But before 1850 there was no punctuation in the manuscript copy of an Act which received the Royal Assent, and it does not appear that the printers had any statutory authority to insert punctuation thereafter. So even if punctuation in more modern Acts can be looked at (which is very doubtful) I do not think that one can have any regard to punctuation in older Acts. And omitting the comma I would hold that the whole of the penalty was subject to modification under the Act of 1842. There is now no comma in s 25(3)(*b*) and in my view, if proceedings are now taken before the General Commissioners they are entitled to reduce the penalty of treble tax.'

Fowler gives, in his book, a comprehensive list of the misuses of the comma. The following are instances of its correct use:

(1) A comma is primarily used to insert a pause into a sentence so as to break it up into articulate phrases or clauses.

(2) A pair of commas may operate in the same manner as a pair of dashes or brackets.

(3) In reported speech, before a person's name, a comma is inserted eg: 'Would you like some refreshment, Mr Micawber?'

(4) A comma is inserted before 'but', where 'but' is used to change direction: 'The European Court ruled that

the granting of an exclusive manufacturing or production right in one Member-State may be justified
to support investment in new technology, but not the
granting of exclusive selling rights'.

(5) A comma is used to separate defining clauses (which
do not need a comma between the item and its definition) as distinct from describing clauses (which do
need a comma between the item and its description):
'He offered me a distributor's agreement which does
not interest me, whereas an exclusive manufacturing
licence, which he knew I wanted, he said was no longer
available'.

8.06 Pair of commas treated as parentheses

In *R v Casement* [1917] 1KB 98 (CCA) the court was called
upon to consider the Statute of Treasons 1351 (translated from
the original French) which reads as follows:

> Item, whereas divers opinion have been before this time in
> what case treason shall be said, and in what not; the King,
> at the request of the Lords and of the Commons, hath made
> a declaration in the manner of hereafter followeth; that is
> to say . . . or if a man do levy war against our lord the King
> in his realm, or be adherent to the King's enemies in his
> realm, giving to them aid and comfort in the realm, or
> elsewhere, and thereof be probably attainted of open deed
> by the people of their condition . . .

Accused was alleged, on different occasions in December
1914 and January and February of 1915, to have solicited and
endeavoured to persuade certain persons, being British subjects,
and members of the military forces of the King, and being
prisoners of war imprisoned in a camp in Germany, to forsake
their duty and allegiance to the King, and to join the armed
forces of his said enemies, and to fight against the King and his
subjects.

Lord Reading CJ at p 129: 'In my judgment, the words
"giving to them aid and comfort" may be read as a parenthesis;
yet I do not confine the application of the words "or elsewhere"
to that parenthesis; I think they apply just as much to the
parenthesis as to the words which precede it. My view is,

although it is not necessary to state it for the purposes of this case, that the words "or elsewhere" govern both limbs of the sentence—both the adhering to the King's enemies and the aid and comfort to the King's enemies—and that it is an offence to adhere within the realm or without the realm to the King's enemies, and it is equally an offence to adhere within the realm to the King's enemies by giving them aid and comfort without the realm.'

8.07 Commas treated as rendering a word an alternative

In *Houston v Burns* [1918] AC 337 (HL) a clause in a trust disposition and settlement dated 2 June 1894, directed that the residue of the settlor's estate should be disposed of as she should direct by any writing or codicil under her hand. The following words were included: 'And failing any such then I hereby direct my Trustees to hold such residue until such time or times as they see fit and apply the same for such public, benevolent, or charitable purposes in connection with the parish of Lesmahagow or the neighbourhood.'

Lord Finlay LC at p 340: 'No direction in writing or by codicil was given by the testatrix, and the question arises whether the bequest for public, benevolent, or charitable purpose is good . . .' at p 341; 'It was contended, however, on behalf of the appellant that the clause should not be read as applying to public or benevolent or charitable purposes, but that on its true reading it was for the benefit of benevolent or charitable purposes of a public nature in connection with the parish. . . . It appears to me that without the punctuation which appears in the will as printed in the appendix this is a quite possible construction, and where words are ambiguous a construction should be adopted which will not make the bequest void. But we are informed that the comma after the word "public" and that after the word "benevolent" appear in the original will, and this points plainly to the conclusion that "public" was intended as an alternative to "benevolent or charitable". In other words, that the clause must be read disjunctively. . . . It follows that the bequest is bad for uncertainty.'

8.08 Single dashes

The dash should not be used as a substitute for the more appropriate form of punctuation, as is sometimes done by those nor sure of themselves on matters of punctuation.

Traditionally, it is a horizontal line at mid-letter level, longer than a hyphen and interposed between words without spacing. A hyphen may be used instead in which case a space appears before and after the hyphen. It may be used in place of a colon and for the same purposes: it is not followed by a capital letter.

It is considered to be useful for the purpose of marking hesitation, parentheses, interruptions, abrupt turns of thought, passages used in explanation, the springing of a surprise at the end of a sentence, and summing up what had gone before.

8.09 Pairs of dashes

These are used, among other instances, for the interjection of an explanation usually in confirmation of what would be assumed. They are preferably not used as an alternative to a pair of brackets.

8.10 Hyphens

Fowler says that the uses of hyphens are infinite. One use (in addition to showing a break in a word which has to be parted for typographical purposes, to maintain a right-hand margin in text), is to make nouns from phrasal verbs or compounds:

> The game analogy suggests that these things are fun, pastimes or what-have-you.

> They thought that all honest-to-john meaningful propositions were either analytic or synthetic.

> It was a wash-out.

> There was a take-over of the company.

> He was a ne'er-do-well.

8.11 Brackets

Brackets are equivalent to a footnote. They are for the purpose of containing an aside which needs to be known if the substance of the sentence in which they occur is to be fully appreciated. A pair of commas or dashes is an alternative. Brackets have the advantage over dashes in that brackets always come in pairs whereas dashes do not: the reader therefore knows the significance of the first bracket, but not necessarily of the first dash.

8.12 Exclamation marks

These should be confined to exclamations such as 'oh!' for example. They should not be used to emphasise an emotionally charged sentence.

8.13 Double quotation marks in either form

The present convention appears to be that double quotation marks are used to indicate words actually spoken, and the titles of books and other works, whilst single quotation marks indicate an unusual word or phrase in the context, but the rule is not uniformly accepted. For quotations within quotations the practice varies: some recommend single quotation marks for a phrase within a longer quoted phrase, and others the reverse. Alternatively, use brackets, hyphens, or dashes for separating the internal phrase from the one in which it is incorporated.

8.14 Single quotation marks

These may be used in place of hyphens, to mark a compound expression such as 'forms of life'. (Do not fall into the mistake of writing 'it's', unless you mean the abbreviation for 'it is'. The possessive of 'it' is 'its'.).

8.15 Apostrophe after 's'

The rule is that an apostrophe followed by an 's' is added for the possessive case thus: 'St James's Square, SW1', including the case where the word is a monosyllable as in 'Sitz's work', but excepting the case where the last syllable begins with an 's' as in 'Moses' law. Most biblical or classical names such as Jesus, Thucydides, Euripides are also exceptions to this rule. There are however further exceptions, and it seems that one may take into account how the construction would sound when spoken. For example, 'Achilles' heel', 'Pears' soap', and other similar cases, which would pose a problem over the speech form, if the strict rule were to be observed.

8.16 Plural anomalies

These are dealt with in more detail by Fowler in his book and include such words a 'Deeds Poll', 'will-o'-the-wisps', 'gins-and French' and 'whisky-and-sodas'.

8.17 Plurals and possessives

The word 'money' has the plural 'monies'. The possessive can it seems take either of two forms: 'money's-worth' or 'monies'-worth', each having a slightly different connotation, and hence, application.

8.18 Relationship between stops and quotation marks

The conventional rule has been that stops come within the inverted commas. Fowler regards this as illogical. The question is whether you should write:

(a) 'He called it "the House of Fear".' or

(b) 'He called it "the House of Fear." '

This is a point of nicety on which practices differ. The former seems the more logical. Similar problems arise with exclamation marks or question marks. The former again would seem to be preferable.

8.19 Standard practices

There are certain standard practices used by printers and publishers, which may afford a useful guide in cases of doubt. These are as follows:

(1) *Commas* are used to separate a series. Where there is a list of items they are normally separated by commas, where the list is inclusive, as in: 'fish, meat, poultry and game', or where it is discrete, as in 'cut, bend or break'.

(2) *Semicolons* separate complete clauses, or sentences within one sentence. A semicolon so used is not followed by a capital letter.

(3) *Colons* are used to add to a sentence or phrase another sentence or phrase which follows from what is contained in the first phrase, such as a conclusion or deduction. In the case of a concluding sentence, it may begin with a capital. In the US this is the practice.

(4) *Brackets* are best avoided where one phrase is to be contained within another bracketed phrase: use hyphens for the innermost phrase, or quotation marks. Brackets are however used, if within a quotation something is to be interjected, as where part is emphasised by the person quoting, and not contained within the original, when one would insert '[emphasis added]'.

(5) *Apostrophes* show the possessive case and they may also be used in certain forms of plural. In the singular possessive the apostrophe comes before the 's' or 'x' as in John's book' and 'Ajax's shield' but, note 'Achilles' heel'. In the case of the plural possessive the apostrophe comes after the word and the 's' is usually omitted as in 'publishers' proofs' and 'witnesses' statements'. Note that in the case of single letters and coined phrases, one uses an apostrophe only if it is required to make clear that the 's' is to produce a plural, for example is it not required in 'the three Rs', and 'several YHAs', or 'the 1980s', but it is required in 'mind your p's and q's', and 'do's and don'ts'.

(6) *Numbers* are best spelt out up to ninety-nine. Beyond that, use figures, unless the number must begin a sen-

tence, when it should be spelt out, but it is preferable that one should reconstruct the sentence so that the number is not at the beginning. The comma used to show 1,000 is not used for dates or page numbers. Unless fractions are essential, use decimals. Different rules apply in respect of the following: percentages, ratios, statistics, chapter numbers, sections and page numbers, degrees in temperature, weight, area, hours and street numbers, among others.

8.20 Capitals

In relation to capitals, it is again difficult to lay down any principle. Apart from the well-known rule that proper names should have a capital letter as the first letter, and that includes not only the names of people, but also of places such as towns and counties, it is reasonably safe to limit the use of capitals to the particular, and use lower case for the general. This usually results in a subsidiary rule that capitals may be appropriate in the singular, and lower case in the plural. Thus, if you wish to refer to something which happened in the 'English Parliament' you would use capitals, whereas if you were to refer to the 'trappings of parliaments', lower case would be acceptable and, generally speaking, appropriate. A rule of thumb is: when in doubt do not begin a word with a capital letter. It is interesting today to look at eighteenth-century statutes with their spattering of capitals throughout the text, and to see how ugly the general appearance is to modern eyes.

Part II

Structure and Composition

Chapter 9

Document Checklists

Checklists of proposed clauses serve two useful functions: they help ensure that you have not overlooked a possible clause in an agreement to be drafted, and they assist in devising a logical order to the clauses, so that the agreement reads logically.

Preparation of a checklist prior to drafting is therefore a useful exercise. A number of representative examples are given below, and in the second part of this section will be found exercises in structuring a clause after the checklist has been determined.

Two general areas are considered at the outset.

9.01 Exclusion clauses

For an exclusion clause to serve its purpose it must not only be effectively incorporated into the contract but must be apt to cover the particular loss or damage which has arisen; be capable of withstanding the courts seeking to give full effect to the clause (particularly by use of the doctrine of fundamental breach); be lawful; and avoid being void and of no effect under statute.

Such advice is beyond the compass of this work and the reader is referred to Richard Lawson's excellent work *Exclusion Clauses* (Longman) 1990.

9.02 Boilerplate clauses

These clauses are common to nearly all commercial contracts and deal with the way in which the contract itself operates.
  (1) Designation of parties
  (2) Successors and assigns
  (3) Extensions of the parties eg subsidiaries

(4) Territories (particularly the EEC)
(5) Periods of time
(6) Scope of undertakings
(7) References to recital clauses and schedules
(8) Commencement and termination
(9) Confidentiality and disclosures
(10) Intellectual property rights
(11) Standard warranties, guarantees and indemnities
(12) Exclusions of liability
(13) Retention of title and vesting
(14) Service of notices
(15) Whole agreement and variation clauses
(16) Disputes and conflict of laws.

For a discussion of the negotiation, drafting and effect of these clauses the reader is referred to Richard Christou's indispensable book *Boilerplate: Practical Clauses* (Longman) 1990.

It hardly needs to be said that it is advisable to set out clauses in a reasonably logical order. Examples are given below in key areas of drafting.

9.03 Conveyancing

Checklists set out below cover:
(1) Contract for the sale of registered land
(2) Transfer
(3) Contract for sale of unregistered land
(4) Conveyance.

It is assumed in each case that the property is freehold and that there is one seller and one buyer.

(1) Contract for sale of registered land incorporating standard conditions of sale (freehold: 1 seller: 1 buyer)
(1) Date
(2) Parties
(3) Incorporation of standard conditions
(4) Agreement to sell and price
(5) Deposit and holder
(6) Capacity of seller
(7) Vacant possession on completion

(8) Statement of freehold and Land Registry number
(9) Incumbrances
(10) Inspection of the Register
(11) Deed of Transfer to contain terms in Schedule
(12) Completion date
(13) Prescribed rate of interest
(14) Sale of fittings
(15) Definition of working days
(16) Exclusion of specific standard conditions
(17) Designated banks

(2) Transfer (of whole freehold 1 seller: 1 buyer)

(1) District
(2) Title number
(3) Property
(4) Date
(5) Payment, receipt and transfer
(6) Indemnity covenant
(7) Certificate of value.

(3) Contract for sale of unregistered land incorporating standard conditions of sale (freehold: 1 seller: 1 buyer)

(1) Date
(2) Parties
(3) Incorporation of standard conditions
(4) Agreement to sell and price
(5) Deposit and holder
(6) Vendor's capacity
(7) Vacant possession on completion
(8) Statement of freehold and root of title
(9) Conditions
(10) Completion date
(11) Prescribed rate of interest
(12) Sale of fittings
(13) Definition of working days
(14) Exclusion of specific standard conditions
(15) Designated banks.

(4) Conveyance (freehold: 1 seller: 1 buyer)

    (1) Date
    (2) Parties
    (3) Recital
    (4) Payment, receipt and conveyance
    (5) Indemnity covenant
    (6) Acknowledgement for production of documents and undertaking for safe custody
    (7) Certificate of value
    (8) Witnesses.

Further detail and variation is available from *Practical Conveyancing Precedents* by Trevor Aldridge (Longman).

9.04 Wills and probate

The checklist set out below is that for an absolute residuary gift:

    (1) Revocation
    (2) Appointment of executors and trustees
    (3) Specific legacies
    (4) Pecuniary legacies
    (5) Personal chattels legacy
    (6) Definition of my estate
    (7) Administration of my estate
    (8) Absolute residuary gifts
    (9) Executors powers
    (10) Schedule (administrative powers)
    (11) Testimonium and attestation.

It should be borne in mind that a more complicated will may require additionally:

    (1) Residuary gifts containing
        (*a*) an absolute gift with gifts over in trust
        (*b*) a life interest with gifts over in trust and powers of advancement
        (*c*) an overriding power of appointment
        (*d*) a life interest with gift over on accumulation and maintenance trusts
        (*e*) a protective life interest with gifts over in trust and powers of advancement

(2) Discretionary trusts

(3) Accumulation and maintenance trusts

(4) Charitable trusts.

There are in addition subsidiary documents including deeds of variation, deeds of disclaimer, appointments under settled legacy or trusts of residue, appropriation and memoranda of wishes. Only the most common is dealt with here:

(1) Codicil

(2) Declaration

(3) Schedule (details of prior codicils)

(4) Testimonium and attestation.

The reader is referred for greater detail to the *Will Drafts-man's Handbook* (Longman) 1990, and *Practical Will Precedents*.

9.05 Lease

(1) Grant by landlord and acceptance by tenant for specified time from an agreed date at the rent stated

(2) Dates or periods when payment of rent due

(3) Tenant's covenant to pay rent together with other outgoings charged on the premises or the occupier

(4) The premises and equipment installed by landlord to be kept in repair and working order by tenant, including painting the exterior for weather protection

(5) Premises to be used as a private dwelling (where applicable)

(6) Landlord covenants for quiet enjoyment by tenant

(7) Right of re-entry by landlord for breach of the terms specifying what is a breach

(8) Right of tenant to terminate tenancy—specifying circumstances giving rise to this right

(9) Provision for service of notice by either party according to the then existing statutory provisions—see Recorded Delivery Service Act 1962 (see *Anns v Merton* [1977] 2 All ER 492)

(10) Provisions concerning legal expenses for preparation of documents.

(1) Residential lease

The following checklist takes into account the short-term lease of a furnished house:

(1) Date
(2) Parties and addresses
(3) Agreement to let defined premises for a fixed term with the commencement date and a specified rent; also payment date and frequency
(4) Responsibilities of tenant eg to pay all rent and bills; keep clean and tidy and in good condition etc
(5) Landlord's covenants eg to indemnify the tenant against water charges; for quiet enjoyment etc
(6) Determination of tenancy on specific grounds eg unpaid rent
(7) Acknowledgement of deposit and agreement to return same
(8) Witnesses.

Residential leases are complicated by the existence of short-hold and assured tenancies and secure tenancies.

Draftsmen should bear in mind that special care will be required for lettings to companies, students, holiday-makers, employees and by resident landlords, owner-occupiers and servicemen. Retirement homes, too, attract specific problems. Charles Bennett's exemplary work *Drafting Residential Leases* should be referred to for a more detailed examination of this subject.

(2) Business lease

The checklist below provides a wide range of clauses that are likely to be encountered or should be included:

(1) Date
(2) Parties
(3) Title
(4) Properly (including rights of access and passage)
(5) Rights
(6) Reservations
(7) Special rights and reservations
(8) Term
(9) Initial rent

(10) Rent reviews
(11) Initial works
(12) User
(13) Repairs
(14) Alterations
(15) Assignment and sub-letting
(16) Insurance and service charges
(17) Costs
(18) Liability of securities

9.06 Trusts

This checklist is for the basic form of an absolute trust:
(1) Date
(2) Parties
(3) Recitals
(4) Definitions
(5) Trust for sale
(6) Trusts of added property
(7) Trusts of capital and income
(8) Trusts for primary beneficiaries under 25
(9) Ultimate default trust
(10) Administrative powers
(11) Extended power of maintenance
(12) Extended power of advancement
(13) Restrictions on powers
(14) Trustee charging clause
(15) Appointment of new trustees
(16) Proper law, forum and place of administration
(17) Exclusion of settlor and spouse
(18) Stamp duty certificate
(19) First Schedule (administrative powers)
(20) Second Schedule (initial trust fund).

9.07 Option

(1) Parties
(2) Offeror offers right to purchase property described
(3) Price of option now paid
(4) How and within what time option to be exercised

(5) Price to be paid for property if and when option is taken up.
(6) How and when completion to be effected
(7) Whether with or without warranties, and if with, stating nature.

9.08 Contract to acquire rights

(1) Exordium and parties
(2) Recital or narrative identifying vendor's mode of, and/or assertion of, acquisition of, or possession of rights and title
(3) Statement of nature of transaction and consideration
(4) Terms of the agreement are:
  (*a*) sale and purchase of property including description thereof identifying it precisely
  (*b*) covenants for title eg as beneficial owner if English law applies
  (*c*) completion arrangements, undertaking to complete documentation and hand over any relevant prior documents or evidence, and any articles or objects
  (*d*) vendor to render any assistance required in perfecting purchaser's title to property
  (*e*) warranty of no outstanding encumbrances
  (*f*) other warranties (if any) relevant to nature of property
(5) No rights granted by vendor to others or held over property by third parties
(6) How notice may be given to be legally effective of any claim by one party over the other arising out of this contract
(7) Law governing contract.

9.09 Computer supply contract

(1) Description of computer including central processing unit employed and memory capacity, operating system and means of storage of data

   (2) Desks, printer stand, or work station to be supplied, storage for tapes, diskettes, manuals etc
   (3) Description of peripherals to be supplied
   (4) Description of software and manuals to be supplied
   (5) Means of safe carriage and delivery
   (6) Provision for testing installation and training of personnel
   (7) Cost and method of payment, whether sale or hire
   (8) Arrangements for servicing and updating of software.

9.10 Joint venture

   (1) First party to acquire firm contract for the project as a condition precedent to the coming into force of the arrangement
   (2) Terms of the contract for the project to be agreed with the other joint venturers
   (3) Specify party to prepare working arrangements assigning duties to each, get out critical path analysis for co-ordination of tasks
   (4) Agree on performance guarantees that may be offered
   (5) Assign co-ordinator for drawings and specifications to be interrelated
   (6) Arrangements for meetings, who should attend
   (7) Exchange of technical data arrangements
   (8) Assign to one party production of computer software to be mutually compatible for design and for any numerically controlled machinery
   (9) Co-operative assistance to be freely given within reasonable limits, arbitration on disputes on this point by the Institute of Mechanical Engineers
  (10) Accountants to be appointed to be responsible for accounts and for calculating profits and shares thereof
  (11) Arrangements for drawings of profits
  (12) Mutual exchange of technical information under secrecy pledges by specified qualified technicians
  (13) Arrangements for safe custody of documentation
  (14) Under what circumstances any party may be dismissed from the project and another appointed in his stead

(15) Whether the rights arising are to be held individually or in common

(16) What warranties if any shall be offered to customer

(17) On conclusion of the project, how arrangements to be wound up.

9.11 Plant and equipment supply agreement

(1) Definitions

(2) Plant and equipment as defined to be delivered giving date and location

(3) Drawings and technical data to be supplied

(4) Confidential know-how to be disclosed or made available

(5) Precautions for keeping know-how secret, custody of drawings and manuals, named personnel to be responsible

(6) Financial provisions

(7) Accounts to be rendered and payments made

(8) Improvements made by either party: how to be disclosed and applied

(9) Dealing with patents that may be granted

(10) Duration and prior termination

(11) Rights arising on termination

9.12 Turnkey contract

(1) Definitions

(2) Description of site where factory and offices to be erected

(3) Conditions precedent to coming into force of agreement

(4) Machinery to be supplied and installed

(5) Training in know-how

(6) Use and safe custody of know-how

(7) Production methods and marketing training

(8) Management arrangements and training

(9) Payments, accounts, exchange rates and methods of transmission

(10) Warranties, performance bonds

(11) Alcohol and firearms prohibited to local labour force
(12) Use of trademarks, licensing
(13) Duration and termination
(14) Force majeure
(15) Conciliation and arbitration
(16) Notices: how served
(17) Proper law applicable to contract

9.13 Franchise

(1) Parties
(2) Description of subject matter of franchise
(3) Establishing and operating
(4) Standard of service and quality of product
(5) Advertising and promotional aids
(6) Trade marks, licensing
(7) Payments, accounting, records
(8) Indemnities, options for extension
(9) Right of assignment
(10) Termination for breach
(11) Loss of rights on termination
(12) Notices
(13) Arbitration
(14) Proper law applicable to contract.

9.14 Agency

(1) Appointment of agent by supplier (or principal) stating whether a sole agency or an exclusive agency, and for what area.
(2) Duration of agency and whether renewable
(3) Duties of agent:
    (*a*) manner of promotion of sales
    (*b*) not to sell goods of competitor of supplier/manufacturer
    (*c*) not to sell goods for re-sale
    (*d*) not to sell goods as loss-leaders
    (*e*) whether credit may be given to customers and limits thereof

(*f*) not to give warranties beyond those granted or agreed by supplier

(*g*) keep proper accounts and allow inspection by supplier

(*h*) to respect trade marks of supplier

(*j*) keep premises in good repair

(*k*) insure premises and stock

(4) Supplier agrees:

(*a*) to supply goods within specified time from receipt of order subject to force majeure

(*b*) Advise agent of sale opportunities

(*c*) Rate of profit on sales

(5) Termination clause for breach, financial failure or force majeure

(6) Duration and orderly termination provisions

(7) Disputes to go to arbitration or to alternative dispute resolution

(8) Service of notices

(9) Proper law.

9.15 Service agreement

(1) Appointment to post described

(2) Period of appointment and whether from year to year, month to month etc or fixed period

(3) Duties to be performed

(4) Renewal of contract if permissible

(5) Remuneration: rate and how paid

(6) Absence for sickness, holidays etc

(7) Employee failure to perform satisfactorily; employer's business failing

(8) Inventions or know-how devised by employee

(9) Duty of employee to observe confidence in relation to business matters

(10) Notice to terminate,or resignation.

Chapter 10

Analysis and Composition of Clauses

The purpose of this section is to look at some typical clauses with a view to arriving at a method of structuring a clause as an alternative to the use of a precedent book, in particular where a suitable precedent is not available for your particular needs. You can structure a clause for a special situation by commencing with the core or basis of the provision, and building upon it according to what is called for in the particular case.

However, before considering that process, it will be helpful to commence by looking at the process of analysing a complex clause into its constituent elements. Thereafter we can tackle the reverse process of building up a clause from the essential elements.

10.01 Analysing complex text

Having discussed, in Part I, the structuring of sentences with a view to producing readable matter, it may be useful to consider the problem of the interpretation of complex provisions. It is a situation with which the lawyer in particular, is often concerned, especially where a client has a problem arising out of the interpretation of, for example, a standard form contract, with complex provisions in small type. A similar problem can arise over the interpretation of some of our statutes after Parliament has hacked at the Bill as drafted by Parliamentary Counsel who have no opportunity or right to re-draft it.

To quote from a government publication written for the Civil Service College, *Occasional Paper No 2: Flow charts, logical trees and algorithms for rules and regulations*: 'As society increases in complexity, rules and regulations proliferate. They also become more complicated and, consequently, less intelligible. Worse still, they impinge upon more and more people who may lack the time or the inclination or the ability to study them.'

10.02 Obscure terminology tolerated

The majority of the population seems to have become so used to the mass of rules and regulations constantly being turned out either by Parliament, or by ministries under their powers to issue regulations, or by traders with their printed form purchase orders, that they no longer attempt to find out the real meaning and impact of the complex terminology. They hope against hope that the verbiage is only concerned with exceptional conditions not likely to be encountered by the average man, or that the terms have been approved by some appropriate body (because that is what ought to be the case).

As mentioned in Part I there is in fact a movement towards clearer terminology in consumer contracts, supported by the Consumer's Association. In the meantime, the lawyer often has to tackle not only complex standard terms and conditions, but also many a statute dealing with some of the more obscure aspects of the law, or a lengthy and complex legal document, hoping to be able to satisfy himself as to its true meaning and intent.

10.03 Use of flow charts and diagrams

The method recommended in the above-mentioned paper comprises up to three steps. The first step, 'decoding the message', may be sufficient in some cases. If not, the second step is to convert the passage into more intelligible prose, and if that is not sufficient, then it may be worthwhile converting the material into an alternative mode of presentation.

> (1) The first step comprises the construction of a table or diagram of the elements contained in the passage, and setting them out in columns and lines according to the relationship between the various elements as laid down in the original clause. The example given in the work referred to above, is taken from a clause relating to capital gains tax where there are three elements, each

of which is capable of being combined in one of six different relationships. This diagram therefore has three columns and six lines covering the elements in the clause, and there is a fourth column showing the resultant calculation that is called for, for each of the six cases.

(2) The second step comprises a restructuring of the original clause based on the diagram prepared in the manner explained above. The result may be unsatisfactory because it will almost inevitably result in a much lengthier passage with a great deal of repetition, so that the intelligibility is likely to be lost in the increased verbiage. It is a matter of trial and error (or success) in each case.

(3) The third step is to construct a diagram or flow chart in which each element is shown in question form, placed in a separate box, and the relationship between the boxes is indicated by arrows. Each arrow has a 'yes' or 'no' set against it, according to whether the answer to the question is or is not provided by the box to which the arrow points. In the example, all boxes have two arrows, one 'yes' pointing to one box, and one 'no' pointing to a different box. Readers who have studied the art of the writing of even simple computer programs will be familiar with the practice. This structure yields a number of answers according to which line of arrows is followed. The result shows the way in which the particular clause operates, and the number of possible combinations, with their solutions.

10.04 An aid to clear thinking

As the authors point out, constructing a flow chart is an aid to clear thinking. It is sometimes referred to as 'a logical tree' or a 'directed graph'. An alternative is the compiling of a list of questions based on the elements to be taken into account in analysing the clause, sometimes referred to as a 'list structure' or 'branching program'.

The preferred generalised terminology for these structures is 'algorithm' as used in computer programming, ie 'an orderly sequence of instructions for solving a problem'.

10.05 Algorithms justified on grammatical grounds

According to the authors of the pamphlet, the use of algorithms for dissecting complex language can be justified on grammatical grounds. Quoting other investigators, the authors report that:

> Research . . . has shown that the time taken to respond correctly to a sentence varies according to its grammatical structure. Affirmative, active, declarative sentences can be most readily processed, and each grammatical transformation generated from these (eg to produce negative or passive sentences) creates additional difficulties which delay correct identification of meaning . . . strings of qualifiers (providing, except, etc) are known to be troublesome . . . As Wason and Jones (1965) point out 'When strings of sentences of differing grammatical structure are inter-related in continuous prose, it seems highly likely that the detrimental effects on comprehension will be cumulative'.

That is perhaps not a very profound conclusion, but it is nonetheless acceptable.

'The advantage of algorithms', say the authors, 'is that they remove the need for words like "if", "but", and "unless". By addressing the reader directly, they can solve his problem without ever departing from syntactically simple questions. In effect, an algorithm is a sort of *adaptive questionnaire* which adjusts its questioning to suit the special needs of the individual'.

10.06 Making an emergency telephone call

Readers of this book are not likely to have any problem in making an emergency telephone call from a call box. Even if they had forgotten, or were a little hazy about, the procedure, it is set out in an orderly manner in a framed notice in the box.

It has been discovered, however, that many people faced with the need to make such a call find the instructions difficult to follow. The authors show how much simpler those instructions would be if they were to be set out in the form of a simple algorithm with straightforward questions in boxes, each box having two arrows, one arrow pointing to a 'no' answer, and telling the caller what to do if the answer to the question in the box is 'no', and a 'yes' arrow telling the caller what to do if the answer to the question is 'yes'.

10.07 Use of algorithms in legal problems

A study of the pamphlet should convince most readers not only of the usefulness of constructing charts, diagrams, question lists or algorithms, in order to analyse a complex clause in a statute or other legal document, but also in their use when structuring a clause which has to cover a complex problem.

For the purposes of this work, a fairly complex statutory provision will be taken as an example. A suitable one is to be found in s 10 of the Copyright Act 1956, as amended by the Design Copyright Act 1968. Indeed, it was the subject of some controversy arising out of the apparent and unexpected width of its operation following the amendment (since replaced by the Copyright, Designs and Trademarks Act 1988).

The section, as amended read as follows (note that subss (1) and 2 (c) had been deleted in the amending statute):

10 Special exception in respect of industrial designs

. . .

(2) Where copyright subsists in an artistic work, and—
  (a) a corresponding design is applied industrially by or with the licence of the owner of the copyright in the work, and
  (b) articles to which the design has been so applied are sold, let for hire, or offered for sale or hire whether in the United Kingdom or elsewhere, the following provisions of this section shall apply.

(3) Subject to the next following subsection, after the end of the relevant period of 15 years it shall not be an infringement of the copyright in the word to do anything which at the time when it was done would, if a corresponding design had been registered under the Registered Designs Act 1949 (in this section referred to as 'the Act of 1949') immediately before that time, have been within the scope of the copyright in the design as extended to all associated designs and articles.

In this subsection 'the relevant period of 15 years' means the period of 15 years beginning with the date on which articles, such as are mentioned in paragraph (*b*) of the last preceding subsection, were first sold, let for hire or offered for sale or hire, whether in the United Kingdom or elsewhere.

(4) For the purposes of subsections (2) and (3) of this section, no account shall be taken of any articles in respect of which, at the time when they were sold, let for hire, or offered for sale or hire, the design in question was excluded from registration under the Act of 1949 by rules made under subsection (4) of section one of that Act (which relates to the exclusion of designs for articles which are primarily literary or artistic in character); and for the purposes of any proceedings under this Act a design shall be conclusively presumed to have been so excluded if—

(*a*) before the commencement of those proceedings, an application for the registration of the design under the Act of 1949 in respect of those articles had been refused;

(*b*) the reason or one of the reasons stated for the refusal was that the design was excluded from such registration by rules made under the said subsection (4); and

(*c*) no appeal against that refusal had been allowed before the date of the commencement of the proceedings or was pending on that date.

(5) The power of the Board of Trade to make rules under section thirty-six of the Act of 1949 shall include power to make rules for the purposes of this section for determining the circumstances in which a design is to be taken to be applied industrially.

(6) In this section, references to the scope of the copyright in a registered design are references to the aggregate of the things, which, by virtue of section seven of the Act of 1949, the registered proprietor of the design has the exclusive right to do, and references to the scope of the copyright in a registered design as extended to all associated designs and articles are references to the aggregate of the things which, by virtue of that section, the registered proprietor would have had the exclusive right to do if—

(*a*) when that design was registered, there had at the same time been registered every possible design consisting of that design with modifications or variations not sufficient to alter the character or substantially to affect the identity thereof, and the said proprietor had been registered as the proprietor of every such design, and

(*b*) the design in question, and every other design such as is mentioned in the preceding paragraph, had been registered in respect of all the articles to which it was capable of being applied.

(7) In this section 'corresponding design', in relation to an artistic work, means a design which, when applied to an article, results in a reproduction of that work.

The elements of s 10 are therefore:

subs (2)

(*a*) An artistic work in which copyright exists

(*b*) A corresponding design that has been 'applied industrially' by or with licence of copyright owner

(*c*) Articles to which design applied are sold etc

subs (3)

(*d*) After the end of fifteen years no infringement of copyright in work to copy the design (as though it had been a registered design). Period calculated from date of first sale of articles

subs (4)

(*e*) Exclude articles which are excluded from registration under Registered Design Act 1949 (ie Design Rule 26); presumption of exclusion if application to register refused for reasons stated

subs (5)

(*f*) Power of Board of Trade to make rules

subs (6)

(*g*) Definition of scope of copyright in design

subs (7)

(*h*) Definition of 'corresponding design'—a design which

when applied to an article results in a reproduction of the copyright work.

The flow chart or algorithm related to the above is given on p 115.

Copyright Act 1956, s 10: Flow Chart

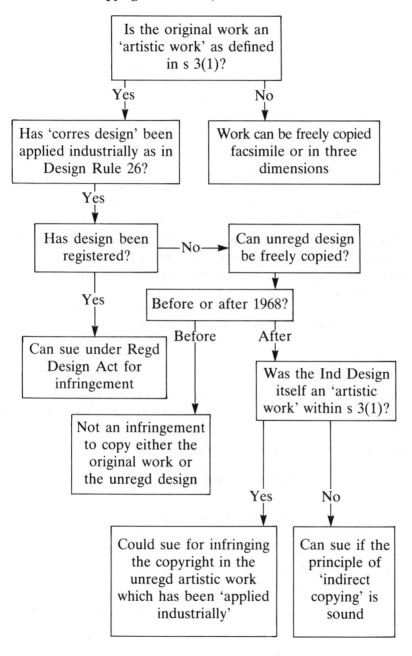

Chapter 11

Structuring a Clause

The following exercises give examples of how to structure a clause, element by element.

11.01 Termination clauses

There are various circumstances which can give rise to a situation where one party wants to terminate a contract against the will of the other. A contract can always be terminated by agreement.

It may be helpful to start with a simple form and consider what additions or qualifications would be desirable: A simple form whereby either party can give notice of termination at any time would be completely without security for either party, and would not normally be acceptable in any contract. Such an arrangement is much too broad for almost any case. Both parties are likely to want a minimum period before which termination could be exercised, and that will normally have been expressed as the duration of the contract. There are therefore possible cases:

(1) setting minimum period before termination can take effect

(2) termination before expiration for breach of the terms and

(3) extension of the original term subject to a reasonable period of termination.

Taking (1) first a possible clause would be:

Either party shall be empowered to terminate this agreement by notice in writing to expire not earlier than the . . . day of . . . and given not less than one month prior to the date when the termination is to take effect.

116

In the case of the second alternative, (2), something along these lines would need to be added:

> Should either party be in breach of any of the terms hereof and fail to remedy the breach (where remediable) within a reasonable time after notice thereof has been given by the aggrieved party, or a time (not being less than one month) stated in the notice, the party serving the notice may terminate this agreement forthwith by a further notice in writing.

In respect of (3), the relevant clause may read:

> On the expiration of the term hereof either party shall be entitled to call for an extension of the agreement on the same terms as the terms hereof for a further period of . . . years by notice in writing given no later than three months before the time when the agreement would otherwise expire.

Alternatively, it may read:

> Should either party wish to renew this agreement prior to its expiration, he shall give notice in writing to the other party stating the terms upon which he is prepared to operate the agreement, such notice to be given not later than six months prior to the date of expiration otherwise applicable to this agreement.

Provision has however not been made for the effect upon the agreement, of the service of a notice to terminate: can the other party during the period of notice carry on as before? If it is a distributorship, and it is the agent who is in default, can the other party continue to place orders? The following may therefore be added:

> Goods and materials ordered during the period of notice will continue to be supplied on a cash with order basis by the Principal.

It may also be necessary to add another phrase, namely:

> Such orders will be executed on condition that the distributor supplies the Principal with a complete list of his customers.

There is yet more to be considered: There is the question of the insolvency of either party, or of the winding up of one of the parties being a company in which event the following may be added:

> Should either party become insolvent, or if a receiver or trustee should be appointed of the assets of either party, or being a company, a resolution for winding up is passed (not being a voluntary winding up) the other party may terminate this agreement forthwith by notice in writing, and such notice shall be deemed validly served if served upon the receiver, trustee or liquidator, or in the case of a company, at the registered office.

If the agreement is with a person or company in another country a further clause might be added:

> If diplomatic relationships between the country of the Principal and the country of the Distributor should be severed and such severance seriously affects the ability to carry on operating this agreement either party shall be entitled to serve a notice giving three months' grace within which to bring the agreement into a state of suspense, and during such suspension neither party shall be deemed to be in breach of the agreement notwithstanding a continuing endeavour to operate the agreement without complying fully with the other terms hereof.

Another possibility is that one of the parties might come under the control, albeit limited, of another company, and it may be thought desirable to provide that if the take-over extends to more than a given proportion of the share capital, right to terminate should be included:

> If the share capital of either party should come under offer to another company to an extent exceeding (twenty) percent and the offeror company is a competitor of the other party, this agreement may be terminated by notice in writing given to expire not earlier than three months from the date of service.

It may also be necessary to consider whether a particular person employed by one party is important to the other party because of his known ability. If he ceases to be employed in the business, there may be a right to terminate, or to suspend the agreement pending his replacement.

Having dealt with the various circumstances in which an agreement may be terminated, the further question arises as to how that termination is to operate:

—Can one party acquire the stocks of goods in the possession of the other party, and if so on what basis?

—If there is a provision relating to advertising must it cease forthwith on service of a valid notice?

—Suppose goods have been supplied to the defaulting party who has not paid for them? May the other party exercise the rights of an unpaid seller to recapture them?

—Shall the payment terms of the agreement be altered so as to require payment either on demand, or within seven days, or indeed shall prepayment with order be stipulated?

—Will either party be entitled, or shall he be expressly disentitled, to compensation for loss of goodwill on termination of the agreement?

11.02 Payments clauses

These clauses are also very important in any agreement. Quarterly accounting is a very common arrangement where payments have to be made by one party to the other in respect of business done. The quarter days will be selected according to what is convenient, and should be expressed in the document.

Provision for proper books of account to be kept should be specified, and those books should be separate from other accounting matters and open for inspection. Vouchers in support of the entries should be preserved and made available, including works orders and invoices. A right to inspect should be reserved, either by the party or his authorised representative being a professionally qualified person.

If the agreement is between persons in different countries one must consider how payment is to be transferred ie in what currency and how conversion is to take place. Shall it take place from day to day at the exchange rates operating daily, or shall sums due be accumulated quarterly and conversion take place on the quarter day? Who shall bear the costs of transmission? Is the payment to be sent by draft through the post, or between the parties' respective bankers?

Part III

Judicial Interpretation

Chapter 12

Judicial Interpretation

12.01 Specific periods of time

The basic rule of interpretation of a provision specifying the hour at which an act is to be done is that calculated from the position of the sun at the place where the event is to be done. Thus the hour at which it is announced that a court will sit will be that applicable at the place where the court is situated. Unless otherwise stated or indicated, the hour of the day for actions or events taking place in the UK will be taken to mean Greenwich Mean Time and not local time (where different) (Interpretation Act 1978, s 9).

That rule is subject to the change occurring during the period of summer time when, unless the contrary is provided, one hour is to be added to Greenwich Mean time (Summer Time Act 1972).

Where time is indicated by reference to the sun eg 'sunrise' or 'sunset', local time will govern the action or happening.

In the case of statutory provisions which have a reference to time the reference is to be interpreted as referring to Greenwich Mean Time as provided in the Interpretation Act 1978 (Summer Time Act 1972).

(1) Quarter day

The four quarter days are determined by reference to the four 'feast days' viz Lady Day (25 March), Midsummer day (24 June), Michaelmas Day (29 September) and Christmas Day (25 December). Half quarter days fall on 2 February, 9 May, 11 August and 11 November.

(2) Day

The draftsman needs to be clear as to the meaning intended to be ascribed to this word as it can mean variously; 24 hours from the first stroke of midnight; a period of 24 hours beginning at the time specified by the draftsman; or the period between sunrise and sunset. The latter is the presumed meaning in the absence of anything to the contrary. A provision dependent upon a person being present for a specified number of days in a year is satisfied if he is present for any part of that day (*Walcot v Botfield* (1854) 69 ER 226). Days are generally consecutive days and the draftsman should consider the use of the expression 'working days', or 'business days'.

(3) Days

Performance, such as payment, due monthly on a particular specified day of the month will be due on that same day each succeeding month, except where the day is the 29th, 30th or 31st and the next month has only 28 days, or, where due on the 31st, the next month has only 30 days; in such cases the last day of the next month will be the day for performance.

Payment 'one month from the 11th' of the month will be due on the 12th of the next month (*Cartwright v MacCormack; Trafalgar Ins Co (Third Party)* [1963] 1 WLR 18 (CA)); equally payment due within a specified number of days of a specified date will be due within that number of days not counting the specified date (*Dodds v Walker* [1981] 1 WLR 1027 (HL)).

The decision in *Trow v Ind Coope (W Mid) Ltd* [1967] 2 QB 899 (CA) concerns the serving of a writ within a year of issue: the writ was issued on 10 September 1965, marked as issued at 3.05 pm and was served on 10 September 1966 before 1.00 pm. Nevertheless, it was out of time since one does not count the first day: the year from the 10 September expires on the 9 September of the following year. The court criticised the then applicable rules of the Supreme Court, which used the expressions 'beginning with the date of issue' since this should not be taken into account and was irreconcilable with the accepted rule. Denning LJ (as he then was) after pointing out that the general rule that one excludes the date from which the period runs, had been laid down in *Lester v Garland* (1808) 15

Ves 248 added 'To distinguish between "beginning with" and "beginning from" is a lawyer's refinement too subtle for practical use.'

The interval of 'not less than fourteen days' which, under the Companies Act 1862 was required to elapse between the meetings respectively passing and confirming a special resolution of a company, is an interval of fourteen clear days exclusive of the respective days of meeting. Therefore a special resolution for reduction of capital held on 25 February 1885 and confirmed on 11 March 1885 was held bad. The year 1885 was not a leap year, otherwise the proceedings would have satisfied the statutory requirement (*Re Ry Sleepers Supply Co* (1885) 29 Ch D 204).

In the Australian case of *Forster v Jododex Australia Pty Ltd* (1972) 127 CLR 421 it has been held that there is a prima facie rule of construction that where a lease or a licence is expressed to commence 'from' a specified day, the term commences at midnight on the day specified, and lasts during the whole anniversary of the day from which it began, unless a different intention is revealed in the document.

(4) Week

A week is normally calculated from midnight Saturday to midnight on the following Saturday, but it may be specifically made to apply from midnight of one specified day of the week, or date, to midnight seven days later.

(5) Month

The term 'month' will normally be taken to mean a calendar month unless otherwise specified (Law of Property Act 1925, s 61(a)). The same rule normally applies where the reference occurs in documents relevant to legal proceedings (*Re A Debtor* [1940] Ch 470; [1940] 2 All ER 303, CA). Where the period of a month is to be calculated from a specified date in a month, the period expires on the same day of the succeeding month.

Thus a bill of exchange payable in a calendar month dated 29 January will be payable on 28 February subject to days of grace, except in a leap year when it will fall due on 29 February (*C A Stewart & Co v P van Ommeren (London) Ltd* [1918] 2 KB 500, CA).

Again, where a calendar month's notice is specified, if the notice is given on 28 April it expires on 29 May (*Freeman v Read* (1963) 4 B&S 174; *Dodds v Walker* [1981] 2 All ER 609).

(6) Year

The expression will usually mean a calendar year (and in a leap year will be 366 days (*R V Worminghall* (1817) 6 M&W 350; 165 ER 1274) but a contract may stipulate a 12 month period to run from any chosen date. In the absence of such a stipulation a calendar year is 1 January to 31 December.

(7) Meaning of 'after 12 months . . .'

This phrase was defined in the case of *Partenreederei MS Karen Oltmann v Scarsdale Shipping Co Ltd (The 'Karen Oltmann')* [1976] 2 Lloyd's Rep 708. The owners of the Karen Oltmann let their vessel Karen Oltmann to the charterers 'for a period of two years 14 days more or less' with an option to redeliver in the following terms: 'Charterers to have the option to redeliver the vessel after 12 months' trading subject to giving three months' notice.'

After trading for nineteen months the charterers gave three months' notice of their intention to redeliver the vessel, upon which the owners protested that the option to redeliver could be exercised only when the vessel had traded for twelve months, so the notice ought to have been given approximately nine months from the date of delivery. There had been a precontractual statement to the effect that 'after 12 months' trading' meant that the charter would be for two years with an option in favour of the charterers to keep the vessel for twelve months only instead of two years.

Mr Justice Kerr: 'This is a case arising out of a Baltime charterparty of a vessel called the Karen Oltmann which raises a short but puzzling point of construction and the old problem whether in cases of doubt it is permissible to refer to the precontract exchanges between the parties . . .

The charter was dated New York, November 5 1969. I first set out part of clause 7, not because anything turns on it, but because it provides some background to the construction of the clauses upon which everything turns.

. . . The charterers to give the owners not less than ten days' notice at which port and on or about which day the Vessel will be re-delivered. Should the Vessel be ordered on a voyage by which the Charter period will be exceeded the charterers to have the use of the Vessel to enable them to complete the voyage, provided it could be reasonably calculated that the voyage would allow re-delivery about the time fixed for the termination of the charter, but for any time exceeding the termination date the charterers to pay the market rate if higher than the rate stipulated herein.

The important provisions are clauses 1 and 26, as follows:

(1) The Owners let and the Charterers hire the vessel for a period of two years, 14 days more or less in Charterers' option. (see clause 26)

(26) Charterers to have the option to redeliver the vessel after 12 months' trading subject to giving three months' notice.

The dispute turns on the meaning of the word "after". The owners submit that "after 12 months' trading" means "when the vessel has traded 12 months" or "on the expiry of 12 months' trading". The charterers submit that it means "at any time after the vessel has traded for 12 months". What happened was this: The vessel was delivered on January 3 1970, and the charter period then began to run. On July 30 1971, when the vessel had traded for about 19 months without any relevant incident, the charterers gave three months' notice of their intention to redeliver the vessel. On this basis she would therefore have been kept in their service for about 22 months, or about two months short of the basic period of the charter. The owners protested and contended that the option of premature redelivery under clause 26 was no longer open at that time. They said that the option of redelivery before the expiry of two years could only be exercised when the vessel had traded for 12 months, and that the necessary notice for this purpose would therefore have had to have been given about nine months from the date of delivery.

It seems to me, and was not really in dispute, that neither the requirement of three months' notice in clause 26 nor the qualification of the basic two year period by 14 days more or less in clause 1 are of any assistance to resolve these contentions. The option is to redeliver prematurely, ie, before the expiry of the two years, and it is in any event subject to three months' prior notice having been given. Furthermore the actual date of redelivery is in any event narrowed down by the provisions of clause 7. One is therefore still left with the question: is the option limited to redelivery at about the time when the vessel has completed 12 months' trading, or is it still open at any time during the following year, in either case subject to three months' prior notice having been given by the charterers?

The answer to this question depends on the meaning which one gives to the word "after". As shown by the dictionary and as a matter of ordinary parlance, although "after" means "later in time", it can be, and is, used in two senses. The intended meaning depends on the context. For instance, if two people embark on a 10 mile walk and agree to have a rest after five miles, they mean that they will have a rest when they have walked five miles and not at any time between five and ten miles. On the other hand, if they take part in a race under rules which say that competitors may take refreshment after five miles, then one would say that the intended meaning is that they can do so at any time after they have covered five miles. But one can also think of many illustrations in which either meaning might be equally defensible. For instance, if someone has a service agreement for 20 years which provides that he may retire on pension after 15 years, it would be very debatable whether he could only exercise this option after 15 years and not, say, after 18 years. This is the sort of point of construction which is largely a matter of first impression in the particular context. I was referred to two cases, one Australian and one Canadian, in which the meaning of "after" was discussed in particular contexts, but they merely illustrate that the meaning depends on the context. My first impression was that the intention of the parties in the present case was that, subject to having given three months' prior notice, the charterers were only to have the option of redelivering the vessel prematurely on the expiry of 12 months' trading and not at any time during the second year. However, as in all cases of first impression, it is difficult to justify the impression. When I search my mind about this, two reasons predominate. Both derive from having considered a large number of charterparties. First, if the meaning for which the charterers contend had been intended, then I would have expected clause 26 to include the words "at any time", which one frequently finds in charterparties, before the words "after 12 months' trading". Secondly, while an option to charterers to terminate a time charter on notice at a certain time within the basic period is by no means unusual, I do not recollect ever having seen one in which the charterers can terminate it on notice at any time, let alone after a certain point of time. In other words, while a charter for either two years or one year at charterers' option has a familiar ring, a charter for a minimum of one year with an option for any period between one and two years seems unfamiliar. My first impression was therefore that this is a charter for a basic period of about two years with an option to the charterers to keep the vessel for about one year only, but not one whereby they can redeliver her at any time during the second year on giving three months' notice. I recognise that this intention could have been conveyed differently and obviously much more clearly, but arguments on these lines can always be raised against a particular construction in doubtful cases. I certainly see nothing strange or unfamiliar in achieving this objective by means of clauses 1 and 26 . . . The first question which arose at this point was whether this plea and submissions founded on it entitled the Court to look at the exchange of telex messages . . .

I think that in such cases the principle can be stated as follows. If a contract contains words which, in their context, are fairly capable of bearing more than one meaning, and if it is alleged that the parties have in effect negotiated on an agreed basis that the words bore only one of the two possible meanings, then it is permissible for the court to examine the extrinsic evidence relied upon to see whether the parties have in fact used the words in question in one sense only . . .

I therefore turn to consider the pleaded telex exchanges. Although I do not consider that they support the allegation of an estoppel, I think that they clearly show that the words "after 12 months' trading" were used in an agreed sense. From start to finish the owners wanted maximum duration and certainty whereas the charterers wanted minimum duration and maximum flexibility. It is clear that both parties throughout used the word "after" in the sense of "on the expiry of" and not "at any time after the expiry of".'

(8) Specified period of time

Where a number of days, weeks or months is adopted in a document as the period relevant to the provision thereof, the day first mentioned is normally excluded (*Webb v Fairmaner* (1838) 3 M&W 473). Should the period expire on a Sunday, that day will not be excluded unless specifically so provided (*Mesure v Britten* (1796) 2 Hy Bl 617; *Dechene v Montreal City* (1894) 9 Exch 730).

Where a limitation period expires on a day when the court office is not open then, for the purpose of legal proceedings, a writ issued on the following day will stand (*Pritam Kaur v S Russell & Sons Ltd* [1973] QB 336; [1973] 1 All ER 617 (CA).

Where a street letter box is provided, it is no excuse not to make use of it on a Sunday if that is the last day for giving notice (*Swainston v Hellon Victory Club Ltd* [1983] 1 All ER 1179; [1983] 1 CR 341, CA).

12.02 Time-related words/phrases

(1) Reasonable time

The interpretation of this expression will depend upon the circumstances and will be interpreted as a question of fact to be answered by reference to all the known circumstances. (*Hick v Raymond & Reid* [1893] AC 22 (HL).

(2) Time of the essence

Failure to perform strictly to time entitles the other party to terminate the contract immediately and without notice. Where it is directly stipulated to be of the essence, or where necessarily implied (per Romilly, MR in *Parkin v Thorold* (1852) 22 LJ Ch 170).

(3) Within . . . days/months

Any date within the delimited period will satisfy such a provision if it immediately precedes the stated date. 'Within' a specified number of days after an event means days exclusive of the day of the event (*Williams v Burgess* (1840) 10 LJ (NS) CL 10).

(4) During

During a stated time will not usually mean in the course of that time but means in strict legal language throughout the whole time; not from time to time in a period but persisting for the whole. See *R v Inhabitants of Anderson* (1846) 9 Ad & El 663 at 668; 115 ER 1428 at 1430.

(5) Until

The word may be construed either exclusive or inclusive of the day to which it is applied according to the context or subject matter (*R v Stevens* (1804) 5 East 244; 102 ER 1063: *Pugh v Duke of Leeds* (1777) 2 Coup 714; 98 ER 1323). It is generally interpreted to exclude the first day and to include the last day to which it is prefixed.

In arbitration matters 'until' will generally include the whole of the day named (*Kerr v Jeston* (1842) 1 Dowl NS 538; 45 Itals 1127).

(6) Before

The draftsman is put on notice that 'before' may be held to mean 'immediately before'.

'Before marriage' or 'before her marriage' does not mean 'before ever having been married', but 'before the marriage existing at the time her liability is under consideration' (*Jay v Robinson* (1890) 25 QBD 467; CA).

'Before' in bankruptcy law means 'next before' (*Re Smith ex p Fox* (1886) 17 QBD 4).

(7) After

The day of the event will be excluded in the computation of a period described as being after an event (*Williams v Burgess and another* (1840) 10 LJQB 10 (Denman CJ); *Robinson v Waddington* (1849) 18 LJQB 250).

Where a time has to expire after an event prior to the doing of some other act, or the happening of an event, the time is to be clear time (*Browne v Black* [1911] KB 975).

(8) Immediately

The word implies that an act should be done with all convenient speed (cf forthwith, there being no material difference in meaning of these two words).

'To make good the deeds and intent of parties it shall be construed such convenient time as is reasonably requisite for doing the thing.' The words 'then and there immediately' held not to exclude all mesne acts (*R v Francis et al* (1735) Can 155; 94 ER 1123).

(9) Meaning of 'forthwith'

'Forthwith' was defined in the case of *Re Van der Jagt (a debtor)* (1960) NZLR 149 Sup Crt, where it was ruled that Service which is to be 'forthwith' in a statute is a directory admonition, not a mandatory one.

F B Adams J: 'Section 37(2) of the Bankruptcy Act 1908 requires that a copy of the summons and petition "shall forthwith be served upon the debtor" . . . after the filing of the petition and the issue of the summons.

Mr Somers . . . contended in reliance on the decision of the English Court of Appeal in *Re A Debtor* . . . [1939] Ch 251, and in particular on a passage in the judgement of the learned Master of the Rolls, Sir Wilfred Greene (ibid 256) that, as in the case of a writ, the requirements of the law in regard to the service of a bankruptcy petition must be regarded as strictissimi juris. In my opinion that case has no application here . . .

It is true that the petition in the present case was served only a short while before the time fixed in the summons for the hearing; but any embarrassment that might have been occasioned to the debtor by the delay in the service of the petition has been mitigated or removed by the adjournment of the case . . .

As to the meaning of "forthwith" in s 37(2) I need do no more than refer to the discussion of that word by Sim J in *Re Olsen* (1919) NZLR 73, 76, where he expressed himself to the effect that a reasonable latitude is permissible in its interpretation. The same view is, indeed, implicit in *Re Neale* (1928) GLR 75, where a strict interpretation would necessarily have led to a contrary decision.

But, apart from any question of reasonable latitude in interpretation, there is also a question whether a failure to serve within the proper limit of time, whatever that limit may be, will necessarily render the proceedings void; or, in other words, whether the direction that service is to be effected "forthwith" is mandatory or directory. If it were mandatory, then it would follow that a bankruptcy petition must necessarily be dismissed if service has not been effected within such a time as can reasonably be regarded as coming within the meaning of the word "forthwith". It is obvious that in *In Re Neale* Sir Charles Skerrett CJ, though he made no express reference to the point, did not regard the provision as mandatory; and I respectfully agree with that view. The distinction between directory and mandatory provisions is well established and depends in every case on the construction of the particular statute, it being always a question whether the preliminary requirement is intended by the legislature to be a condition precedent to the jurisdiction or not. An illustration may be found in the case of *Scott v Scott* (1924) NZLR 191; (1924) GLR 208 in which the provision of the Divorce and Matrimonial Causes Act 1908, requiring that there should be filed with a petition an affidavit negativing collusion or connivance had not been complied with, the affidavit not having been filed until the day before the hearing. It seems to me that s 37(2) is as readily capable of being construed in the directory sense as was the provision considered in *Scott v Scott*. It is not to be supposed that every breach of a statutory requirement will render proceedings void.'

Alternatively, 'forthwith' may mean within a reasonable time as in the case of *Re Southam, Ex p Lamb* (1881) 19 Ch D 169.

An appeal by the trustee in bankruptcy against a refusal to make a bankruptcy order on 12 July was entered by the London agents of the trustee's solicitors, who were in Manchester. They entered it in London and should have lodged a copy 'forthwith' with the solicitors to the respondents.

It was established that the London Bankruptcy Court closes at 4 pm on a Friday, and the office of the county court closes at 1 pm on Saturday. Letters for night mail from London to Manchester can be posted as late as 7 pm. The office of the London agents to the trustee's solicitors was in the City.

The notice of appeal was lodged on 5 August, Friday. A copy

was received by the trustee's solicitors at Manchester on Monday by post from their London agents, and they sent a copy to the Registrar of the county court who did not receive it until after Monday, the last day.

Lush LJ at p 173: 'The word "forthwith" has not a fixed and absolute meaning; it must be construed with reference to the objects of the rule and the circumstances of the case. In the present case the Appellants had not to wait to do the act till someone asked them to do it; it was simply their duty to do it. The entry of the appeal in London and the giving of notice to the Registrar in the country were one continuous act, which was to be done within a reasonable time. I do not think the letter was posted within a reasonable time when the Appellants lost the three hours from 4 to 7 pm on the Friday within which it might have been posted.'

(10) Days of grace

Three days, called 'days of grace', are added (unless otherwise specified) to the time of payment for a bill (Bills of Exchange Act 1882, s 14).

(11) 'On' or 'from' a date

This phrase is defined in *Sidebotham v Holland* [1895] 1 QB 378 where an agreement was expressed as 'commencing on the 19th of May, 1890' and provided for an apportioned rent to be paid up to the next quarter day forthwith, and future rent to be payable in advance on the quarter days.

On 17 November 1893 the landlord gave a notice to quit on 19 May next. Held: The notice was valid.

Lindley LJ at p 382: 'It is true that, if the tenancy commences on May 19, the last quarterly payment to be made in advance on the previous Lady Day will not be a full quarter's rent, but only a proportionate part of it—viz an apportioned part for the time which will intervene between Lady Day and May 19. But this circumstance only shows that the agreement is not very accurately drawn. The inaccuracy does not justify the conclusion that the tenancy did not commence on the day expressly mentioned for its commencement—viz on May 19, 1890; and that the time which intervened between that day and June 24 was not part of the tenancy. Treating the tenancy then as commencing on May 19, 1890, the question is whether a notice to quit on May 19, 1894, given by the landlord on November 17, 1893, is a good notice. It is a six calendar months' notice to quit on the anniversary of the day on which the tenancy commenced. Why, then, is it bad? The notice is said to be bad because it expires one day too late. The contention is that, as the tenancy commenced "on" the 19th and not "from" the 19th, the notice should have been to quit on the 18th and not on the 19th . . .' at p 384: 'When considering the validity of a notice to quit given in time and expiring on the anniversary of the commencement of a tenancy, I can find no distinction ever drawn between tenancies commencing "at" a particular time or "on" a particular day and "from" the same day. "At", "on", "from" and "on and from" are for this purpose equivalent expressions. Any distinction between them for such a purpose as this is far too subtle for practical use. See *Doe d Strickland v Spence* (1805) 6 East 120. In an action for double rent it is, however, necessary to be more particular: *Page v More* (1850) 15 QB 684. So it is when the number of days has to be counted. In the absence of authority compelling me to decide differently, I hold that the objection that the notice was bad because it was a notice to quit on the 19th instead of the 18th of May untenable.'

12.03 Parties

Infant/minor

The word 'infant' was, by tradition, used of a person under 21 years of age. Under the Family Law Reform Act 1969, the terminology was extended to allow the use of the word 'minor' instead of 'infant' (by s 12), and the age at which a person ceases to be a minor is the attainment of his/her 18th birthday. Under s 3 amendments are made to the application and interpretation of earlier statutes relating to wills made after the coming into force of the 1969 Act. Thus, for the words 'twenty-one years' there is substituted 'eighteen years'; further, in the case of intestacy of a person dying after the commencement of this Act, there is to be substituted 'eighteen years' in place of 'twenty-one years' in relation to any statutory trust on intestacy as referred to in s 47 of the Administration of Estates Act 1925.

There is a further provision under the 1969 statute whereby any will made by a person under the age of 18 and being valid under the provisions of s 11 of the Acts of 1837 and 1918 may be revoked by that person notwithstanding that he is still under that age and whether or not the circumstances are such that he would be entitled to make a valid will under those provisions.

By s 9 of that Act it is provided that the time at which a person attains a particular age expressed in years shall be the commencement of the relevant anniversary of the date of his birth, but this provision only applies where the relevant anniversary falls on a date after that on which this section comes into force, and, in relation to any enactment, deed, will or other instrument, has effect subject to any provision therein.

In the case of illegitimate children, it is provided by s 14 that where either parent dies intestate as respects any of his property, the illegitimate child (or, if he is dead, his issue) shall be entitled to take any interest therein to which he or such issue would have been entitled, if the child had been born legitimate; and there are appropriate amendments to the Administration of Estates Act 1925 (Part IV). The definition of 'illegitimate child' does not include a legitimised person, or any adopted person adopted under an adoption order.

There are exceptions: certain statutory provisions relating to 'infants' are unaffected by Sched 2 provisions: these exceptions include provisions relating to voting rights under the Representation of the People Acts, Parliamentary Elections Act 1695, Local Government Act 1933 and any statutory provisions relating to income tax, capital gains tax, corporation tax and estate duty.

The rule applies for any rule of law, and, in the absence of a definition or indication to the contrary intention, it applies to the construction of 'full age', 'infancy', 'minor', 'minority' and similar expressions in

- (a) Any statutory provision whether passed before or after the date on which the section comes into force, and
- (b) any deed, will or other instrument or whatever nature (not being a statutory provision) made on after that date.

There are exceptions: certain statutory provisions relating to 'infants' are, by Sched 2, unaffected. These exceptions include provisions relating to voting rights under the Representation of the Peoples Acts, Parliamentary Election Act 1695, Local Government Act 1933 and any statutory provision relating to income tax, capital gains tax, corporation tax and estate duty.

There are special provisions relating to wills or codicils made before the date of the coming into force of this Act: a will or codicil made before the coming into force of the Act is not affected by reason of its being confirmed by will or codicil made on or after that date.

(2) Child

The interpretation of this word over the past centuries has not been uniform (as may be expected). In the earlier statutes the courts showed a reluctance to include illegitimate children as within the provisions applicable to children (*R v Maude* (1842) 2 Dowl (NS) 58 at 62/3).

Generally, the word, by itself, will normally be interpreted as referring to a legitimate, or legitimised person, including an adopted child whose adoption occurred before the date of the document being interpreted. If, however, the only possible application of the provision would require it to be interpreted more widely, the court may adopt the broader interpretation, and, if necessary, apply it to include an adopted child, an illegitimate child or a stepchild.

For the purpose of certain statutes such as the Employment of Women, Young Persons & Children Act 1933, 'child' means a person under 14 years of age.

In 1845 Lord Denman CJ said 'The law does not contemplate illegitimacy. The proper description of a legitimate child is "child". Again, in 1873, Lord Cairns ruled that the *prima facie* meaning of 'child' is legitimate children and if therefore there are, in the particular case, illegitimate children as well, they will not be included as children to whom the provision applies. However, his Lordship recognised two classes of case where that interpretation would be departed from. The first case is where in the circumstances it is not possible that legitimate children could take under a bequest in favour of 'children'. The second case is where, on a proper interpretation of the words used, it is apparent that a testator intended to use the word 'children' to include any child whether legitimate or not (*Hill v Crest* (1873) LR 6 HL 265).

By 1892 this narrow view was widened to some extent when North, J said: 'I do not see how I am to avoid holding that where, in a gift to children, there being both legitimate and illegitimate children, there is an exception of one of the illegitimate children: the word "children" is intended to include both classes.' (*R v Lowe, Danily & Platt* (1892) 61 LJ Ch 415 at p 417.)

In the case of *Re Milwards Estate ex p Midland Rly Co* [1940] Ch 698, Farwell J, observed: 'Prima facie the words "child or children" mean what they say; but, as a matter of construction of a particular will, it is open to the court, if it thinks fit to do so, to give them a wider meaning.'

It has been argued that a distinction should be drawn between adopted children and illegitimate children on the basis that the adopted type is not the natural child of the parties whereas the illegitimate is a natural child of the parties. Roxburgh, J, refused to apply such an interpretation on the basis that it is common for people to speak of both illegitimate children and adopted children as 'children' *simpliciter* (*Re Fletcher, Barclays Bank v Ewing* [1940] 1 All ER 732, at 735/6).

(3) Agent

Defined by *Halsbury* as 'one who has authority express or implied, to act on behalf of another, called the "principal" and consents so to act'.

(4) Distributor

Defined by s 3 of the Consumer Product Safety Act 1972 as 'a person to whom a consumer product is delivered or sold for purposes of distribution in commerce, except that such term does not include a manufacturer or retailer of such product'.

(5) Servants

Defined in *Re Hudson ex p Homberg* (1842) 2 Mont D&DG 642 thus; 'I do not know of any actual case of a seaman being held to be a servant—but, as he is hired to render his services for certain wages, and he is bound to obey the orders of the master of the vessel who hired him, I think he is as much a servant as the clerk or shopman of any merchant or tradesman'.

(6) Heirs

Since 1925 in the UK, after the abolition of descent to the heir on intestacy, under the Administration of Estates Act 1925, this word lost its earlier meaning which challenged the right of a person to dispose of his real estate by will. See *Gittings v McDermott* (1834) 2 My&K 69; 39 ER 870.

(7) Successors in business

See *R v IRC* [1907] 1 KB 108.

(8) Assigns

The word 'assign' does not mean heir; it means a person substituted for another by an act of some kind and, as the devisee has not done any act to appoint an assignee, the property must go to his administrators (*Doe d Sophia Lewis* (1842) 9 M&W 662; 152 ER 280).

(9) Buyer

This is 'a person who buys or agrees to buy' (Sale of Goods Act 1979, s 61).

(10) Seller

This is 'one who sells or agrees to sell' (Sale of Goods Act 1979, s 61(1)).

(11) Groups of companies

See Income and Corporation Taxes Act 1970, s 280 (7) — this may consist of companies some or all of which are not resident in the UK.

12.04 Commands

(1) 'May'

In the case of *Sheffield Corporation v Luxford* [1929] 2 KB 180 DC, it was held that 'may' in this instance meant 'must' even though the word was permissive in form.

Whatever its meaning in other circumstances, in this case, where a legal right in the plaintiffs was established 'may' was an enabling word, and it was the duty of the judge to exercise the power entrusted to him in the plaintiff's favour.

Also, in the case of *Barnhart v US* (1983) 563 F Supp 1387, the inconsistent use of the words 'shalt' and 'may' were held to equal 'may'.

In that case, the plaintiff, a customhouse broker, whose licence had been suspended, moved for a rule that a three-judge panel should be assigned to hear the case, in particular the contention that the term 'disreputable' is so vague a criterion as to be unconstitutional. The court pointed out:

(1)   Section 255(a) of the relevant statute provides that upon application of any party to a civil action, or upon his own initiative, the chief judge of the Court of International Trade shall designate any three judges of the court to hear and determine any civil action in which the chief judge finds (a) raises an issue of the constitutionality of an Act of Congress, a Proclamation of the President or an Executive order; or (b) has broad or significant implications in the administration or interpretation of the customs laws.

(2)   Rule 77(d) provides (a) that all actions shall be assigned to a single judge except as prescribed in para (2) of subdivision (a); (b) an action may be assigned by the chief judge to a three-judge panel either upon motion, or upon his own initiative, when the chief judge finds that the action raises an issue.

(3)   The plaintiff's claim arises from what appears to be an inconsistency between s 255 and r 77(d).

(4)   Congress' use of the term 'shall' in and of itself does not necessarily require the conclusion that mandatory action is intended. Rather 'as against the government, the word "shall", when read in statutes, is to be construed as "may" unless a contrary intention is manifest': *Railroad Co v Hecht* 95 US 168, 170, 24 L Ed 423 (1877) . . .

The judicial determination, whether a statutory provision is directory or mandatory, involves a consideration of a number of factors . . . No universal rule can be laid down for the construction of statutes, as to whether mandatory enactments shall be considered directory or obligatory. It is the duty of the Courts of Justice to try to get at the real intention of the legislature by carefully attending to the whole scope of the statute to be construed . . .

To achieve legislative purpose and policy of the Customs Courts Act 1970, it is clear that the word 'shall' must be interpreted as permissive, and must be read with the words 'which the chief judge finds'.

(2) 'Must'

In *Posner v Collector for Interstate Destitute Persons (Victoria)* (1947) 74 CLR 461, must was defined at 490: ' "Must" is a word of absolute obligation and occurs in a section which is concerned with a fundamental principle of justice. It is not merely directory.'

(3) 'Permit'

In *Sefton v Tophams (No 2)* [1967] AC 50 (HL), the definition of 'permit' arose as follows. Purchasers covenanted with vendor not to 'cause or permit' the land purchased to be used otherwise than for special purposes, nor to cause or permit buildings to be erected (except an hotel) to be used otherwise than as a private dwellinghouse.

The purchaser parted with the land to a development company and that company acted in a manner which would have amounted to a breach if it had been done with the permission of the vendor.

Lord Upjohn at p 75: I would think that outside the sphere of purely polite language, the word 'permit', used even between laymen bent on serious business or other affairs intended to have legal consequences, would be used as a word connoting on the part of the one whose permission is asked the right effectively to refuse and on the part of the applicant the necessity to ask for and obtain permission, so as lawfully to undertake his proposed course of action. This in my view, is its legal meaning . . . something more is required than mere knowledge of the purchaser's intention to constitute permission.

What have Topham's done to permit the use of the racecourse for some purpose other than racing or agriculture? The truth of the matter is that, whatever their knowledge of the intentions of Capital, they have done nothing to permit such use. They have granted Capital no permission to do anything in derogation of the obligations to which they are themselves subject and to which they themselves have subjected Capital. The vital point, in my view, is that the sole reason why Capital, if the contract is completed, can ignore the covenant is that the Respondent is unable to enforce against Capital the provision subject to which it has agreed to purchase. Capital . . . will be enabled to develop the land not by virtue of any permission given by Topham's but by the inability of the Respondent to enforce any covenant against it.

'Permit' was also defined in *Burton v Alliance Economic Investment Co* [1922] 1 KB 742 (CA) at 759: 'To my mind the word "permit" means one of two things, either to give leave for an act which without that leave could not be legally done, or to abstain from taking reasonable steps to prevent the act where it is within a man's power to prevent it.'

(4) 'Shall'

'Shall' is defined in *A-G Lock* (1744) 3 Atk 164; 26 ER 897 thus: 'The words shall and may in general acts of Parliament, or in private constitutions, are to be construed imperatively.'

(5) 'Will'

'Will' is defined in *Hector SS Co v VO Sovfracht, Moscow* [1945] KB 343.

'In a charterparty a provision for extension of time contained the phrase "Should the steamer be ordered on a voyage by which the charter period will be extended . . .". In the judgment of this case the court ruled that it was immaterial whether or not the word "will" means "shall" and held that the provision related to what is inevitable.'

12.05 Contractual words

(1) Meaning of 'accident'

This word was defined in *Whetsell, Mary H v Mutual Life Ins Co of NY* 669 F 2d 955 (1982). The plaintiff, a widow, claimed against the Insurance Company under an accidental death policy in respect of the death of her husband in hospital caused by the insertion of an infected intravenous needle. Since the use of an intravenous needle was part of the medical treatment, it was not covered by the provision in the policy whereby the insurer did not assume risk for a death caused or contributed to by the treatment or operation for diseases or bodily infirmity.

Chapman Circuit Judge: 'Whetsell was covered by four life insurance policies issued by Mutual. Each policy provided for double recovery in the event of accidental death. The relevant portions of the policy are as follows:

"Accidental death" means death occurring (a) directly and independently of all other causes, as a result of accidental bodily injuries, (b) within 90 days after the date of the accident causing such injuries, and (c) from a cause not mentioned under "risks not assumed".

Risks not assumed: Under this rider the Company does not assume the risk of death caused or contributed to, directly or indirectly, by disease, by bodily or mental infirmity, or by treatment or operation for disease or bodily or mental infirmity . . .

There is no South Carolina case interpreting an exclusionary provision similar to the one presented in this case. We must, therefore, construe the provision in the light of the expressed policy of the South Carolina Supreme Court of strictly construing ambiguities in insurance contracts against insurers. *Hann v Carolina Casualty Co* 252 SC 518 167 SE 2d 420 (1969) . . .

The case most similar to the facts of the present case is *Reid v Aetna Life Ins Co* 440 F Supp 1182 (SD Ill 1977) since aff'd 588 F 2d 835 (7th Cir 1978). In *Reid* the decedent, while recuperating from surgery, received antibiotics intravenously, carried by a saline solution. After two injections of the proper fluid, a poison was inadvertently substituted for a saline solution causing decedent's death . . . The court held that the death fell within the exclusionary provision of the policy stating:

> There can really be no doubt that the death here involved was a direct consequence of medical treatment, ie the administration of keflin to control possible post-surgical infection, as prescribed by the physician. The accidental use of a killer drug as a carrier of the intended drug, in place of normal saline solution as such carrier, whether such use was negligence amounting to medical malpractice, or an unavoidable act of God, or something in between, though obviously not prescribed, would not have occurred but for the treatment, and thus was a consequence thereof. Even though it be

considered that the accidental death was not caused or contributed to by the intended medical treatment, it was caused by the 'accident' which occurred in the course of administering medical treatment.

To come to a conclusion different from that of the *Reid* court would render the exclusionary provision meaningless. Death is never caused by medical treatment absent some misdiagnosis or mistake. Though death may result where proper medical treatment is unsuccessful, death in those cases is caused by preexisting infirmity, not medical treatment. Since all deaths caused by medical treatment necessarily involve mistreatment, to say that mistreatment is not covered by the exclusion is to say that the provision excludes nothing.

Death must be caused by an accident before the accidental death benefits of the policy come into play. An accident is an unintended occurrence. If such happens during medical treatment, it is still an accident, but it is not a risk assumed by the insurance company under the terms of the policy. The use of an infected IV needle was not intended, therefore, it was an accident. However, this occurred as a part of medical treatment, so it is excluded by the clear language of the policy.'

(2) 'Agree'

This was defined in *Clifton v Palumbo* [1944] 2 All ER 497 (CA) as follows: '. . . if you say that the price has been agreed when the contract is being negotiated, you do not use the word "agree" in the sense that any binding contract has been entered into.'

(3) Meaning of 'condition'

This word was defined in the case of *Schuler (L) AG v Wickman Machine Tool Sales Ltd* (1974) AC 235 (HL).

Whether a clause in a document, stated to be a 'condition' will be enforced on the basis that it is in fact a condition, is a matter of construction of the document. Held: That the clause purporting to be a condition was not, as a matter of construction, a condition.

Clause 7(a) provided that Wickman would use its best endeavours to promote and extend the sale of Schuler products, and 7 (b)(i) provided that it shall be a condition that Wickman shall send its representatives to visit six firms listed in the schedule at least once every week.

Lord Reid at p 249: 'I think it right first to consider the meaning of clause 11 because, if Wickman's contention with regard to this is right, then clause 7 must be construed in the light of the provisions of clause 11. Clause 11 expressly provides that the agreement "shall continue in force (unless previously determined as hereinafter provided) until" December 31 1967. That appears to imply the corollary that the agreement shall not be determined before that date in any other way than as provided in clause 11. It is argued for Schuler that those words cannot have been intended to have that implication. In the first place Schuler say that anticipatory breach cannot be brought within the scope of clause 11 and the parties cannot have intended to exclude any remedy for an anticipatory breach. And, secondly, they say that clause 11 fails to provide any remedy for an irremediable breach however fundamental such breach might be.

There is much force in this criticism. But on any view the interrelation and consequences of the various provisions of this agreement are so ill-thought out that I am not disposed to discard the natural meaning of the words which I have quoted merely because giving to them their natural meaning implies that the draftsman has forgotten something which a better draftsman would have remembered. If the terms of clause 11 are wide enough to apply to breaches of clause 7 then I am inclined to hold that clause 7 must be read subject to the provisions of clause 11. . . .

So the question is whether a breach of Wickman's obligation under clause 7(b)(i) is capable of being remedied within the meaning of this agreement. On the one hand, failure to make one particular visit might have irremediable consequences, eg a valuable order might have been lost when making that visit would have obtained it. But looking at the position broadly I incline to the view that breaches of this obligation should be held to be capable of remedy within the meaning of clause 7. . . .

Schuler maintains that the word condition has now acquired a precise legal meaning; that particularly since the enactment of the Sale of Goods Act 1893, its recognised meaning in English law is a term of a contract any breach of which by one party gives to the other party an immediate right to rescind the whole contract.

In the ordinary use of the English language "condition" has many meanings, some of which have nothing to do with agreements. In connection with an agreement it may mean a pre-condition: something which must happen or be done before the agreement can take effect. Or it may mean some state of affairs which must continue to exist if the agreement is to remain in force. The legal meaning on which Schuler relies is, I think, one which would not occur to a layman: a condition in that sense is not something which has an automatic effect. It is a term the breach of which by one party gives to the other an option either to terminate the contract or to let the contract proceed.

Sometimes a breach of a term gives that option to the aggrieved party because it is of a fundamental character going to the root of the contract, sometimes it gives that option because the parties have chosen to stipulate that it shall have that effect. . . .

In the present case it is not contended that Wickman's failure to make visits amounted in themselves to fundamental breaches. What is contended is that the terms of clause 7 "sufficiently express an intention" to make any breach, however small, of the obligation to make visits a condition so that any such breach shall entitle Schuler to rescind the whole contract if they so desire. . . .

The fact that a particular construction leads to a very unreasonable result must be a relevant consideration. The more unreasonable the result the more unlikely it is that the parties can have intended it, and if they do intend it the more necessary it is that they shall make that intention abundantly clear. . . . But if Schuler's contention is right failure to make even one visit entitles them to terminate the contract however blameless Wickman might be.

This is so unreasonable that it must make me search for some other possible meaning of the contract. If none can be found then Wickman must suffer the consequences. But only if that is the only possible construction.

If I have to construe clause 7 standing by itself then I do find difficulty in reaching any other interpretation. But if clause 7 must be read with clause 11 the difficulty disappears. . . .

In my view that is a possible and reasonable construction of the contract and I would therefore adopt it. The contract is so obscure that I can have no confidence that this is its true meaning but for the reasons which I have given I think that it is the preferable construction. It follows that Schuler was not entitled to rescind the contract as it purported to do. So I would dismiss this appeal.'

(4) Covenant'

In *Re Hollis' Hospital Trustees and Hague's Contract* [1899] 2 Ch 540 the issue of a significant effect upon title caused by a covenant void for perpetuity arose.

In 1726 H conveyed land to trustees upon trust for the hospital subject to a proviso that if at any time thereafter the premises or the rents thereof should be employed to any other purpose the premises should revert to H's heirs.

In 1898 the trustees agreed to sell part of the property of the hospital and in the course of the transaction they received a letter from an heir of H objecting to the sale. The writer, the heir, was also a trustee of the hospital.

The intending buyer sought a declaration that a good title had not been established by the hospital. Held: The condition was void at common law as contrary to the rule against perpetuities; and that as the heir declined to be bound by the court's ruling, the title was not one that an unwilling purchaser could be required to accept.

Byrne J at p 549: 'It is laid down in *Sheppard's Touchstone* p 120 that a condition may be annexed to a limitation of uses and thereby the same—namely, the uses or the estates arising from the uses—may be void . . .' at p 551: 'The next question is, whether or not the condition, being an express common law condition subsequent, is void for perpetuity. I have not been referred to any case deciding the question, nor have I since the argument, after a considerable search, been able to find any authority in the reports enabling me to say that the point has been judicially decided.

For the exposition of our very complicated real property law, it is proper in the absence of judicial authority to resort to the textbooks which have been recognised by the Courts as representing the views and practice of conveyancers of repute . . .' at p 555: 'I am of opinion that the condition in question is obnoxious to the rule against perpetuities.

But this still leaves another question for consideration, namely, is the title one which ought to be forced upon a purchaser? . . . Upon a consideration of all the circumstances I do not think I ought to say that such a title has been shewn as ought to be forced upon the purchaser if he is unwilling to complete.'

The issue of a breach of covenant being a matter for opinion of covenantee arose in *Zetland (Marquess) v Driver* [1938] All ER 158 (CA). In a transfer of settled land there was included a covenant to be observed by the transferee in these terms: 'no act or thing shall be done or permitted on the said land which in the opinion of the vendor may be a public or private nuisance or prejudicial or detrimental to the vendor and the owners or occupiers of any adjoining property or to the neighbourhood'; 'vendor' included successors in title.

On the death of the vendor the first plaintiff became entitled as tenant in tail male to the unsold part of the settled land. One of the properties was sold to the defendant and he and another used it as a fried fish shop for consumption off the premises.

In 1936 the first plaintiff, being of the opinion that the user was detrimental to the amenities of the neighbourhood and to his own property, brought a claim to restrain the defendants from inter alia using any part of the premises for frying fish.

Held: Since the first plaintiff was not in any sense exercising a judicial function, or a quasi-judicial function, in arriving at his opinion, he was under no obligation to allow the defendants to argue the matter, or to be heard.

(5) Meaning of 'delivery'

'Delivery' was defined in the case of *Beesly v Hallwood Estates Ltd* [1960] 2 All ER 314.

In the grant of a 21 year lease there was included an option of renewal for a further period of 21 years on giving notice specifying terms to be complied with. The defendant company, owner at the time when the option could be exercised, had acquired freehold and had actual notice of the option, but the option was not registered under the Land Charges Act.

The plaintiff gave notice of exercise of the option for renewal, whereupon the defendant demanded that the premises be re-decorated.

The defendant company's solicitors sent the counterpart lease to the plaintiff for execution by the plaintiff which she did on the 24 or 25 September 1958.

The lease was sealed by the defendant company prior to September 26 when the board of the company met. At that meeting it was questioned whether the company was bound to grant the renewal. It was resolved not to issue the grant of the renewed lease.

Buckley J at p 325: 'The sealing of a deed by a corporate body, in my judgment, prima facie imports delivery of that deed, either unconditionally or conditionally . . . and I see no reason in the present case to conclude that the sealing of the lease by the defendants did not import delivery so as to consti-tute execution either unconditionally or in escrow. Indeed the plaintiff being a "purchaser" within the meaning of the Law of Property Act 1925 I think that I am bound by section 74 of that Act to treat the lease as having been duly executed by the defendants, and this, in my judgment, involves treating the lease as having been not only sealed but also delivered. The lease, being a deed intended to be executed in duplicate for giving effect to a transaction between the parties whereby each under-took obligations towards the other, was, in my opinion, executed by the defendants conditionally on the plaintiff execut-ing a counterpart: the critical question, however, is whether it was also conditional on an undertaking being given in suitable form by the plaintiff in respect of the decorations . . . the seal is countersigned by Mr Scammell who was the chairman of the board meeting of Sept 26, 1958 and the minute of that meeting . . . contains no reference to the execution of the lease being in any way conditional on an undertaking being given by the plaintiff as to decorations. On the contrary . . . everybody . . . regarded the lease sealed by the defendant com-pany as binding, albeit they did so with regret . . . I, therefore, reach the conclusion of fact that the defendants, by sealing the lease, intended to deliver, and did deliver, as their deed intended to bind them, conditionally only upon the plaintiff executing the counterpart, and subject to no other condition.'

(6) Objective test of parties' intention against 'factual matrix'

In *Plumb Brothers v Dolmar (Agriculture) Ltd, The Times* April 7, 1984 (CA) Lord Justice May stated: 'There is a recent tendency to speak of construing documents against the "factual matrix". That was the modern way of saying that one had to look at all the circumstances at the time of the transaction. The true intention of the parties was to be determined from the words of the documents themselves in the light of the circumstances surrounding the relevant transaction.'

(7) 'Guarantee'

In *Seaton v Heath* [1899] 1 QB 782 (CA), 'guarantee' is defined thus: 'A guarantee is an accessory contract whereby the promisor undertakes to be answerable to the promisee for the debt, default or miscarriage of another person.'

In *Fell v Goslin* (1852) 7 Exch 185; 155 ER 909 the phrase 'We guarantee . . . in the proportion of' was held to signify several liability. A contract provided: 'In consideration that you will sell to Mr F the distillery situate at etc and will take Mr F's acceptance to be dated 29 September 1849 for £400 and interest payable at six months after the date, we undertake and guarantee that the said sum of £400 and interest shall be duly paid to you when the said acceptance arrives at maturity in the proportion of £200 each.

Held: Defendants were severally liable to the Plaintiff to the extent only of £200 each.

(8) Principle of interpretation of a statute

This issue arose in *Prenn v Simmonds* [1971] 1 WLR 1381 (HL). Lord Wilberforce at p 1384: 'I may refer to one other case to dispel the idea that English law is left behind in some island of literal interpretation. In *Utica City National Bank v Gunn* (1918) 118 NE 607 the New York Court of Appeals followed precisely the English line. Cardozo J in his judgment refers, at p 608 to "the genesis and aim of the transaction" . . . Surrounding circumstances may, he says, "stamp upon the contract a popular or looser meaning" than the strict legal meaning, certainly when to follow the latter would make the transaction futile. "It is easier to give a new shade of meaning to a word than to give no meaning to a whole transaction." The whole judgment, as one may expect, combines classicism with intelligent realism . . .' at p 1385: 'The words used may, and often do, represent a formula which means different things to each side, yet may be accepted because that is the only way to get "agreement" and in the hope that disputes will not arise. The only course then can be to try to ascertain the "natural" meaning. Far more, and indeed totally, dangerous is it to admit evidence of one party's objective—even if this is known to the other party. However strongly pursued this may be, the other party may only be willing to give it partial recognition, and in a world of give and take, men often have to be satisfied with less than they want . . .

In my opinion, then, the evidence of negotiations, or of the parties' intentions, and *a fortiori* of Dr Simmonds' intentions, ought not to be received, and evidence should be restricted to evidence of the factual background known to the parties at or before the date of the contract, including evidence of the "genesis" and objectively the "aim" of the transaction.'

(9) Meaning of 'may require'

This definition appears in *Parker v Ministry of Transport* (1982) 1 NZLR 209 CA Wellington. The Transport Act 1962 contains provisions under which an enforcement officer 'may require' a driver to submit to certain tests or to go to some other place for the purpose of a test.

Woodhouse P at p 210: 'But in the close context of that subsection the word "may" cannot be read as merely permissive. Instead it points to a power which in any normal situation is intended to be used in favour of the requirement subject only to the single condition which introduces the subsection. The mandatory word "shall" has not been used but that is simply because an immediate test might not be possible for some run of the mill reason such as absence or malfunction of a testing device or ought not to proceed because of some plain and pressing reason such as injury or sudden ill health.'

McMullin J at p 212: 'In a series of decisions . . . Judges in the High Court have expressed different opinions upon what it is that is required of an enforcement officer before he "may require" a suspect to undergo a test . . . At one end of it some Judges have held that these words "impose a discretion" on the enforcement officer which a court can consider as validly exercised only when . . . he exercised it in an independent and unfettered way. At the other end of the spectrum Judges have taken the view that the word "may" in the phrase "may require" means no more than "entitled to" . . . Other views have been expressed within the spectrum some Judges seeking a via media.'

(10) Uncertainty and no case to answer

The issue of 'no case' appears in *National Trust v Midlands Electricity Board* [1952] 1 Ch 380. The owners of common lands agreed to impose on those lands restrictive covenants for the benefit of Midsummer Hill and for the purpose of preserving the amenities of the Malvern Hills, owned by the National Trust. Two covenants were imposed as follows:

(1) No act or thing shall be done or placed or permitted to remain upon the land which shall injure, prejudice, affect or destroy the natural aspect and condition of the land;

(2) No building shall at any time hereafter be erected upon any part of the land by or with the consent of the covenantors.

The Electricity Board began to erect on the land, poles to carry electric cables. Plaintiffs sought an injunction against such work being done.

Vaisey J at p 384: 'What is to be the criterion of such alteration of the natural aspect and condition of the land? There is no such qualification as might have been introduced by such words as "in the opinion of the National Trust" . . . a qualification which would appear to have been accepted as sufficient in the case of *Zetland (Marquess) v Driver*. . . . It is, no doubt, easy to suggest some acts or things which could come within the prohibition—if, for instance, the land were ploughed up or turned into a car-park. . . . The difficulty is to ascertain the limits of the prohibited acts. . . . Counsel for the National Trust during the hearing was driven to admit that the placing of a basket for litter on a short pole, or a seat or a bench, would amount to a breach of the condition. . . .

The fact is that, in my judgment, the omission of any criterion by which these vague and uncertain words can be brought under some control is fatal to the validity of the restriction. I think it is void for uncertainty; it is so vague that it is really impossible of apprehension or construction, and in my judgment is wholly unenforceable. . . . If, however, I am wrong both as to the unenforceabilty of the condition and as to the absence of any relevance in its terms to what has actually happened, there is the further difficulty as to how any restriction so worded can be said to benefit or protect Midsummer Hill. The nearest of these poles to Midsummer Hill is at least 1,100 yards distant from it. No doubt the poles are visible from Midsummer Hill on a reasonably clear day but the effect of their presence or absence from the landscape must be infinitesimal.'

(11) Effect of recital

This is dealt with in *Re Moon, Ex p Dawes* (1886) 17 QBD 275. A debtor executed a deed of composition which recited that he was possessed of or entitled to the real and personal estate specified in a schedule to the deed. The operative part assigned to the trustee 'all and singular the several properties, chattels, and effects set forth in the schedule hereto, and all the estate, right, title, interest, claim, and demand,' of the debtor 'in, to, and upon the said chattels, properties, and effects, and all other the estate (if any)' of the debtor.

Held: General words are controlled by a recital and thus in this case the deed was intended only to apply to the property set forth in the schedule.

Lindley LJ at p 288: 'Any one accustomed to legal documents must be very much struck with the parcels in this deed; I never saw, and I do not suppose anyone else ever saw, such an enumeration. The first part of the description is, "all and singular the several properties, chattels, and effects set forth in the schedule hereto". Of course the words "in the schedule" shew pretty clearly what is meant; there is no ambiguity about it. Then comes what is known as the "all the estate" clause, which is intelligible enough to persons accustomed to legal instruments. Then comes something which strikes one as very odd and incomprehensible. Apart from the recitals we should not know what was meant—"and all other the estate (if any) of the said William Moon". It does not say in what, and, if there were no recitals to throw light upon it, I do not know that anyone could make out the meaning of it. . . . If there was nothing to explain these words, I cannot help thinking that the whole thing would be extremely ambiguous. But the ambiguity is removed at once when you look at the recitals.'

Lopes LJ at p 289: 'There are several well-established rules applicable to the construction of deeds. One is this, that, if the operative part of a deed is clear, and the recitals are not clear, the operative part must prevail. Again, if the recitals are clear, but the operative part is ambiguous, the recitals control the operative part. If, again, the operative part and the recitals are both clear, but the one is inconsistent with the other, the operative part must prevail.

Now we are not asked to rectify this deed; we are only asked to construe it, and the question is, whether Dawes, the trustee of the deed, is an assignee of the debtor's life interest under the settlement. It appears to me perfectly plain that the operative part of the deed is ambiguous. If that is so, then, according to the rules of construction to which I have alluded, it becomes necessary to look at the recitals. And the recitals are as clear as they can well be. There is only one possible meaning.'

(12) 'Undertake'

In *Re Stewart* (1889) 41 ChD 494, it was stated—' "Undertaking any business" means not merely accepting the retainer, but rather entering upon the work'.

(13) 'Warrant'

In *R v Garry* [1882] 9 QBD 93 the term 'warrant' is defined to 'include any judicial document authorising the arrest of a person accused or convicted of crime'.

12.06 Adjectives

(1) Meaning of 'ambiguous'

In *Richard Plantation Co Inc v Justiss-Mears Oil Co Inc* 671 F 2d 154 (1982) (CA 5th Cir) 'ambiguous' is defined as follows.

Under Texas law, a contract is 'ambiguous' when, after applying established rules of construction, it is reasonably susceptible of more than one meaning.

Tate Circuit Judge: 'This Texas diversity suit involves the construction of an agreement to pay an additional (or overriding) royalty in the event of production, beyond that provided by a mineral lease entered into the same day between the parties. The defendant producer-lessee ("Justiss") appeals from the district court's ruling that additional royalty payments are due to the plaintiff landowner-lessor ("Richland") under the additional-royalty agreement. Justiss, the appellant defendant, principally contends that the district court erred in finding ambiguity in the additional-royalty agreement, if construed together with the simultaneously executed lease, and in thus admitting extrinsic evidence to prove the intent of the parties.

We affirm, finding (a) that the district court correctly held that the agreement was ambiguous and that extrinsic evidence was properly admissible to aid in its construction and (b) that the district court was not clearly erroneous in its finding that the parties intended that the additional royalty not be subject to the proportionate reduction clause of the lease that was applicable to royalties provided by the lease itself . . .

    (1) A contract is ambiguous when, after applying established rules of construction, it is reasonably susceptible to more than one meaning . . .

    (2) Under Texas law, the determination of whether or not a contract is ambiguous in order to permit extrinsic evidence of intent is a question of law. Once the contract is found to be ambiguous, however, the determination of the parties' intent becomes a question of fact . . .

    (3,4) When faced with a question relating to the construction of a contract, Texas courts will take the wording of the instrument, consider the same in the light of the surrounding circumstances, and apply the pertinent rules of construction thereto and thus settle the meaning of the contract . . . When several documents represent one agreement, all must be construed together in an attempt to discern the intent of the parties, recon-

ciling apparently conflicting provisions and attempting
to give effect to all of them, if possible . . .

By the lease executed on November 11 1975, the
lessee Justiss agreed to pay the landowner-lessor Richland a one-eighth royalty on all oil and gas produced
from the described land, but (applicable, since Richland
owned only one-half of the mineral interest) the printed
lease form also contained a "proportionate reduction"
clause, which provided:

> If lessor owns a less interest in the above-described
> land than the entire and undivided fee simple
> estate therein, then the royalties and rentals herein
> provided shall be paid to Lessor only in the pro-
> portion which Lessor's interest bears to the whole
> and undivided fee.

Simultaneously with the execution of the lease, Justiss and Richland executed a letter agreement, as
"unrecorded supplement to said lease" which provided:

> In the event production is actually obtained from
> the subject tract or from adjacent property with
> which all or a portion of the subject tract has
> been pooled or utilized to create a producing unit,
> Justiss-Mears Oil Co Inc will assign to Richland
> Plantation Co an additional royalty of seven and
> one half percent of eight-eighths of the oil, gas or
> minerals produced and sold from said well. The
> assignment shall be effective only as to that por-
> tion of the subject tract included within a produc-
> ing unit.

In the district court, both parties moved for summary
judgment, on the contention that the two instruments
construed as a single agreement unambiguously
reflected their respective opposing contentions.

Richland, the landowner-lessor, points out that the
reduction clause applied only to the royalties "herein
provided" by the lease itself ie to the one-eighth primary royalty. Richland argues that the additional royalty letter agreement was supplemental to the lease and
that it specifically provided with regard to this specific
issue, itself not regulated by the lease, that the

additional or overriding royalty would be "seven and one-half percent of eight-eighths" of the mineral production ie of the entire mineral production, not just of the one-half thereof attributable to Richland's one-half mineral interest.

On the other hand, the producer-lessee Justiss contends that the simultaneously executed letter agreement was specifically denoted as "supplemental to" the lease and that, as such, it was subject to all the clauses thereof regulating the payment of royalties, allegedly including the proportionate reduction clause. Justiss argues that, because the letter agreement allegedly incorporated all the royalty provisions (except fractional share) of the original lease, it was unnecessary to specify that the proportionate reduction clause affected the overriding royalty provided by the supplemental agreement (ie as well as the primary royalty provided by the lease itself).

(6) The matter is not free from doubt. We were initially inclined to agree with Richland that the related but self-contained letter agreement with specific regard to the payment of additional royalties in the event of production unambiguously provided that such additional royalties (unlike the primary royalty) was to be based on the entire eight-eighths of the mineral production. Ultimately, however, we are unable to hold that the district court was in error when it found that the instruments construed together were ambiguous (ie had two reasonable susceptible meanings), in so far as providing the proportionate reduction clause did apply to the additional overriding royalty as well as to the primary lease royalty. In reaching this conclusion, we take into consideration the entire instructions and the unexplained (on their face) circumstance that the percentage of overriding royalty would be paid on the entire mineral production of the tract (rather than on the production attributable to Richland's one-half mineral interest).

(7) Based upon the parol testimony as to the perfection of the lease and simultaneously-executed overriding-

royalty letter agreement, substantial evidence supports
the district court's finding that the contractual intent
was that the additional or overriding royalty percentage
was to be based on the entire eight-eighths mineral
production, not just half the mineral interest attributable to it.'

(2) 'Due'

In *Cort v Winder* (1844) 1 Coll 320; 63 ER 438 it is stated that
in a will '. . . the words due or payable are referable to the
time of the testator's death'.

(3) 'Reasonable'

In *Booth v Clive* (1851) 10 CB 827 'reasonable' is taken to
mean 'according to his reason' as distinct from caprice.

12.07 Prepositions

(1) 'Between'

In *Re Harper* [1914] 1 Ch 70, 'between' is defined as a division
into two.

(2) 'In logic there is no rule which requires that "or" should carry an exclusive force'

This issue arises in *Federal Steam Navigation Co v Department
of Trade & Industry* [1974] 1 WLR 505 (HL). The owners and
master of a British ship were each charged with discharging fuel
oil into the sea contrary to the Oil in Navigable Waters Act
1955, whereby it is provided that 'if any oil . . . is discharged
from a British ship registered in the UK into a part of the sea
which is prohibited sea area, or if any mixture . . . (of oil &
water) is discharged from such a ship into such a part of the
sea . . . the owner or master of the ship shall . . . be guilty of
an offence'.

Held: By a three to two majority that both the owner and the
master could be charged, the 'or' being construed conjunctively.

Lord Wilberforce at p 520: 'My Lords, it is important to state
precisely what we are asked to decide in this appeal. To say
that what we have to decide is whether "or" is conjunctive or
disjunctive or, putting it more bluntly, whether "or" means

"and", appears to me, with respect, to be a dangerous simplification. It is the meaning of the phrase as a whole that concerns us.

The appellants ask us to say that, in this context, "or" has an alternative and exclusionary sense, so that either the master or the owner is guilty but not both. Thus, once either one or the other has pleaded or been found guilty or, maybe, has been proceeded against, proceedings against the other cannot be brought. This strange result—*modus ponendo tollens*—"See how the fates their gifts allot, if A is guilty, B is not", was rejected by the judge at the trial, and rejected unanimously by the Court of Appeal (Criminal Division) which court pungently pointed out anomalies and absurdities to which it would give rise . . .

In logic there is no rule which requires that "or" should carry an exclusive force. Whether it does depends on the context. So one must ask what, in a legal context, is the meaning of an assertion that "A or B" is to be guilty of an offence? The law is supposed to be certain: the subject is entitled, and presumptively bound, to know what laws, particularly criminal laws apply to him. To say that a law which fails to satisfy these demands is void for uncertainty, is certainly a last resort, but if that conclusion is to be avoided, some intelligible meaning must be found by supplying or substituting, words within the limits of what courts may legitimately do. It seems clear enough that where the law says that something is to happen to "A or B", if what is intended is an exclusionary alternative (ie one but not the other), the law must state either some qualification (by which the affected person may be determined) or must name a third person by whom the choice is to be made . . .

The following seem to be the only possibilities:

(1) The words might mean "the owner or the master whichever is responsible for causing the discharge." This would be intelligible; but it cannot be the meaning here, because the Act evidently creates an absolute offence. In many, if not most, cases it is impossible to find out who caused or was responsible . . .

(2) The words might mean "the owner or failing him (ie if he cannot be found or proceeded against) the master". This would be intelligible though perhaps difficult to apply. It would have the result of letting the

master escape if the owner could be found . . . There
seems no sound policy reason for this . . .

(3) The words might mean something like "the owner or
master at the option of the prosecution". This is, in
substance, what the appellants contend for. But I find
this less acceptable even than the other two.

To say that either A or B—neither of whom may have caused
the discharge, or possess any mens rea—is liable to be pros-
ecuted—at the choice of the Attorney-General or of a government department, with the consequence that once the choice is
made the other is innocent, appears to me to introduce a novel
and offensive principle of law.'

Part IV

Key Statutory Definitions

Chapter 13

Key Statutory Definitions

The following abbreviations are used in this section:

AEA	Administration of Estates Act 1925
AJA	Administration of Justice Act 1982
FLRA	Family Law Reform Act 1969
IA	Interpretation Act 1978
LPA	Law of Property Act 1925
WA	Wills Act 1837

There follows a table of key statutory definitions followed by the relevant acts which contain the definitions themselves.

Key statutory definitions

Words will be found under the relevant statute heading.

administrators	AEA 1925 s 55
administrator	AEA 1925 s 55
bankruptcy	LPA 1925 s 205
beneficial owner	LPA 1925 Sched 2 Pt 1
building purposes	LPA 1925 s 205
capital money	LPA 1925 s 205
child	AEA 1925 s 55
conveyance	LPA 1925 s 205
———	AEA 1925 s 55
court	AEA 1925 s 55
covenants for title	LPA 1925 s 76
death duty	LPA 1925 s 205
———	AEA 1925 s 55
distance	IA 1978 s 8

163

entailed interest	AEA 1925 s 55
estate	AEA 1925 s 55
estate owner	LPA 1925 s 205
feminine	LPA 1925 s 61
gazette	LPA 1925 s 205
gifts to issue	WA 1837 s 33
gifts to spouse	AJA 1982 s 22
illegitimacy	FLRA 1969 ss 14, 15
income	AEA 1925 s 55
incumbrance	LPA 1925 s 205
instrument	LPA 1925 s 205
interpretation	IA 1978 s 20
interpretation of wills	AJA 1982 s 21
intestate	AEA 1925 s 55
issue	AEA 1925 s 55
land	LPA 1925 s 205
——	AEA 1925 s 55
legal estates	LPA 1925 s 205
——	AEA 1925 s 55
legal mortgage	AEA 1925 s 55
legal powers	LPA 1925 s 205
Limitation Acts	LPA 1925 s 205
lunatic	AEA 1925 s 55
majority, age of	FLRA 1969 ss 1, 9
masculine	LPA 1925 s 61
mental disorder	LPA 1925 s 205
mining lease	LPA 1925 s 205
minister	LPA 1925 s 205
month	LPA 1925 s 61
mortgage	LPA 1925 s 205
notice	LPA 1925 s 205
pecuniary legacy	AEA 1925 s 55
person	LPA 1925 s 61
personal chattels	AEA 1925 s 55
personal representative	LPA 1925 s 205
——	AEA 1925 s 55
possession	LPA 1925 s 205
——	AEA 1925 s 55
power to postpone sale	LPA 1925 s 205
prescribed	AEA 1925 s 55

probate	AEA 1925 s 55
probate judge	AEA 1925 s 55
probate rules	AEA 1925 s 55
property	LPA 1925 s 205
――――	AEA 1925 s 55
purchaser	LPA 1925 s 205
――――	AEA 1925 s 55
real estate	AEA 1925 s 55
rectification	AJA 1982 s 20
registered land	LPA 1925 s 205
regulations re notices	LPA 1925 s 196
rent	LPA 1925 s 205
――――	AEA 1925 s 55
repeal and re-enactment	IA 1978 s 17
representation	AEA 1925 s 55
rules of court	AEA 1925 s 55
sale	LPA 1925 s 205
securities	LPA 1925 s 205
――――	AEA 1925 s 55
settled land	LPA 1925 s 205
――――	AEA 1925 s 55
settlement	AEA 1925 s 55
singular	LPA 1925 s 61
statutory owner	LPA 1925 s 205
――――	AEA 1925 s 55
subsidiary vesting deed	LPA 1925 s 205
tenant for life	LPA 1925 s 205
――――	AEA 1925 s 55
term of years absolute	LPA 1925 s 205
――――	AEA 1925 s 55
time of day	IA 1978 s 9
treasury solicitor	AEA 1925 s 55
trust corporation	LPA 1925 s 205
――――	AEA 1925 s 55
trust instrument	LPA 1925 s 205
trust for sale	LPA 1925 s 205
――――	AEA 1925 s 55
trustees for sale	LPA 1925 s 205
trustees of the settlement	LPA 1925 s 205
――――	AEA 1925 s 55

United Kingdom	LPA 1925 s 205
vesting deed	LPA 1925 s 205
vesting instrument	LPA 1925 s 205
vesting order	LPA 1925 s 205
will	LPA 1925 s 205
——	AEA 1925 s 55

Wills Act 1837

(as amended)

33 Gifts to children or other issue who leave issue living at the testator's death shall not lapse

(1) Where—
   (a) a will contains a devise or bequest to a child or remoter descendant of the testator; and
   (b) the intended beneficiary dies before the testator, leaving issue; and
   (c) issue of the intended beneficiary are living at the testator's death

then, unless a contrary intention appears in the will, the devise or bequest shall take effect as a devise or bequest to the issue living at the testator's death.

   (2) Where—
   (a) a will contains a devise or bequest to a class of persons consisting of children or remoter descendants of the testator; and
   (b) a member of the class dies before the testator, leaving issue; and
   (c) issue of that member are living at the testator's death

then, unless a contrary intention appears by the will, the devise or bequest shall take effect as if the class included the issue or its deceased member living at the testator's death.

   (3) Issue shall take under this section through all degrees, according to their stock, in equal shares if more than one, any gift or share which their parent would have taken and so that no issue shall take whose parent is living at the testator's death and so capable of taking.

167

(4) For the purposes of this section —
  (a) the illegitimacy of any person is to be disregarded; and
  (b) a person conceived before the testator's death and born living thereafter is to be taken to have been living at the testator's death.

Law of Property Act 1925

(as amended)

There are a number of sections by which terms are implied as document relating to property. The following are of general interest.

61 Construction of expressions used in deeds and other instruments

In all deeds, contracts, wills, orders and other instruments executed, made or coming into operation after the commencement of this Act, unless the context otherwise requires —
   (*a*) 'Month' means calendar month;
   (*b*) 'Person' includes a corporation;
   (*c*) The singular includes the plural and vice versa;
   (*d*) The masculine includes the feminine and vice versa.

. . .

76 Covenants for title

(1) In a conveyance there shall, in the several cases in this section mentioned, be deemed to be included, and there shall in those several cases, by virtue of this Act, be implied, a covenant to the effect in this section stated, by the person or by each person who conveys, as far as regards the subject-matter or share of subject-matter expressed to be conveyed by him, with the person, if one, to whom the conveyance is made, or with the persons jointly, if more than one, to whom the conveyance is made as joint tenants, or with each of the persons,

if more than one, to whom the conveyance is (when the law permits) made as tenants in common, that is to say:

(A) In a conveyance for valuable consideration, other than a mortgage, a covenant by a person who conveys and is expressed to convey as beneficial owner in the terms set out in Part I of the Second Schedule to this Act;

(B) In a conveyance of leasehold property for valuable consideration, other than a mortgage, a further covenant by a person who conveys and is expressed to convey as beneficial owner in the terms set out in Part II of the Second Schedule to this Act;

(C) In a conveyance by way of mortgage (including a charge) a covenant by a person who conveys or charges and is expressed to convey or charge as beneficial owner in the terms set out in Part III of the Second Schedule to this Act;

(D) In a conveyance by way of mortgage (including a charge) of freehold property subject to a rent or of leasehold property, a further covenant by a person who conveys or charges and is expressed to convey or charge as beneficial owner in the terms set out in Part IV of the Second Schedule to this Act;

(E) In a conveyance by way of settlement, a covenant by a person who conveys and is expressed to convey as settlor in the terms set out in Part V of the Second Schedule to this Act;

(F) In any conveyance, a covenant by every person who conveys and is expressed to convey as trustee or mortgagee, or as personal representative of a deceased person, . . . or under an order of the court, in the terms set out in Part VI of the Second Schedule to this Act, which covenant shall be deemed to extend to every such person's own acts only, and may be implied in an assent by a personal representative in like manner as in a conveyance by deed.

. . .

196 Regulations respecting notices

(1) Any notice required or authorised to be served or given by this Act shall be in writing.

(2) Any notice required or authorised by this Act to be served on a lessee or mortgagor shall be sufficient, although only addressed to the lessee or mortgagor by that designation, without his name, or generally to the persons interested, without any name, and notwithstanding that any person to be affected by this notice is absent, under disability, unborn or unascertained.

(3) Any notice required or authorised by this Act to be served shall be sufficiently served if it is left at the last-known place of abode or business in the United Kingdom of the lessee, lessor, mortgagee, mortgagor, or other person to be served, or, in case of a notice required or authorised to be served on a lessee or mortgagor, is affixed or left for him on the land or any house or building comprised in the lease or mortgage, or, in the case of a mining lease, is left for the lessee at the office or counting-house of the mine.

(4) Any notice required or authorised by this Act to be served shall also be sufficiently served, if it is sent by post in a registered letter addressed to the lessee, lessor, mortgagee, mortgagor, or other person to be served, by name, at the aforesaid place of abode or business, office, or counting-house, and if that letter is not returned through the post-office undelivered; and that service shall be deemed to be made at the time at which the registered letter would be in the ordinary course be delivered.

(5) The provisions of this section shall extend to notices required to be served by any instrument affecting property executed or coming into operation after the commencement of this Act unless a contrary intention appears.

. . .

205 General definitions

(1) In this Act unless the context otherwise requires, the follow-

ing expressions have the meanings hereby assigned to them respectively, that is to say:–

(i) 'Bankruptcy' includes liquidation by arrangement; also in relation to a corporation means the winding up thereof;

(ii) 'Conveyance' includes a mortgage, charge, lease, assent, vesting declaration, vesting instrument, disclaimer, release and every other assurance of property or of an interest therein by any instrument, except a will; 'convey' has a corresponding meaning; and 'disposition' includes a conveyance and also a devise, bequest, or an appointment of property contained in a will; and 'dispose of' has a corresponding meaning;

(iii) 'Building purposes' include the erecting and improving of, and the adding to, and the repairing of buildings; and a 'building lease' is a lease for building purposes or purposes connected therewith;

(iv) 'Death duty' means estate duty . . . and every other duty leviable or payable on a death;

(v) 'Estate owner' means the owner of a legal estate, but an infant is not capable of being an estate owner;

(vi) 'Gazette' means the London Gazette;

(vii) 'Incumbrance' includes a legal or equitable mortgage and a trust for securing money, and a lien, and a charge of a portion, annuity, or other capital or annual sum; and 'incumbrancer' has a meaning corresponding with that of incumbrance, and includes every person entitled to the benefit of an incumbrance, or to require payment or discharge thereof;

(viii) 'Instrument' does not include a statute, unless the statute creates a settlement;

(ix) 'Land' includes land of any tenure, and mines and minerals, whether or not held apart from the surface, buildings or parts of buildings (whether the division is horizontal, vertical or made in any other way) and other corporeal hereditaments; also a manor, an advowson, and a rent and other incorporeal hereditaments, and an easement, right, privilege, or benefit in, over, or derived from land; but not an undivided share in land; and 'mines and minerals' include any strata or seam of minerals or substances in or under any land, and powers of working and getting the same but not an undivided share thereof; and 'manor' includes a lordship, and reputed manor or lordship; and 'hereditament' means any real property which on an intestacy occurring before the commencement of this Act might have developed upon an heir;

(x) 'Legal estates' means the estates, interests and charges, in or over land (subsisting or created at law) which are by this Act authorised to subsist or to be created as legal estates; 'equitable interests' mean all the other interests and charges in or over land or in the proceeds of sale thereof; an equitable interest 'capable of subsisting as a legal estate' means such as could validly subsist or be created as a legal estate under this Act;

(xi) 'Legal powers' include the powers vested in a chargee by way of legal mortgage or in an estate owner under which a legal mortgage or in an estate owner under which a legal estate can be transferred or created; and 'equitable powers' mean all the powers in or over land under which equitable interests or powers only can be transferred or created;

(xii) 'Limitation Acts' mean the Real Property Limitation Acts, 1833, 1837 and 1874, and 'limitation' includes a trust;

(xiii) 'Mental disorder' has the meaning assigned to it by section four of the Mental Health Act, 1959, and 'receiver', in relation to a person suffering from mental disorder, means a receiver appointed for that person under Part VIII of that Act;

(xiv) A 'mining lease' means a lease for mining purposes, that is, the searching for, winning, working, getting, making merchantable, carrying away, or disposing of mines and minerals, or purposes connected therewith, and includes a grant or licence for mining purposes;

(xv) 'Minister' means the 'Minister of Agriculture and Fisheries';

(xvi) 'Mortgage' includes any charge or lien on any property for securing money or money's worth; 'legal mortgage' means a mortgage by demise or subdemise or a charge by way of legal mortgage and 'legal mortgagee' has a corresponding meaning; 'mortgage money' means money or money's worth secured by a mortgage; 'mortgagor' includes any person from time to time deriving title under the original mortgagor or entitled to redeem a mortgage according to his estate interest or right in the mortgaged property; 'mortgagee' includes a chargee by way of legal mortgage and any person from time to time deriving title under the original mortgagee; and 'mortgagee in possession' is, for the purposes of this Act, a mortgagee who, in right of the mortgage, has entered into and is in possession of the mortgaged property; and 'right of redemption' includes an option to repurchase only if the option in effect creates a right of redemption;

(xvii) 'Notice' includes constructive notice;

(xviii) 'Personal representative' means the executor, original or by representation, or administrator for the time being of a deceased person, and as regards any liability for the payment of death duties includes any person who takes possession of or intermeddles with the property of a deceased person without the authority of the personal representatives or the court;

(xix) 'Possession' includes receipt of rents and profits or the right to receive the same, if any; and 'income' includes rents and profits;

(xx) 'Property' includes any thing in action, and any interest in real or personal property;

(xxi) 'Purchaser' means a purchaser in good faith for valuable consideration and includes a lessee, mortgagee or other person who for valuable consideration acquires an interest in property except that in Part I of this Act and elsewhere where so expressly provided 'purchaser' only means a person who acquires an interest in or charge on property for money or money's worth; and in reference to a legal estate includes a chargee by way of legal mortgage; and where the context so requires 'purchaser' includes an intending purchaser; 'purchase' has a meaning corresponding with that of 'purchaser'; and 'valuable consideration' includes marriage but does not include a nominal consideration in money;

(xxii) 'Registered land' has the same meaning as in the Land Registration Act, 1925, and 'Land Registrar' means the Chief Land Registrar under that Act;

(xxiii) 'Rent' includes a rent service or a rentcharge, or other rent, toll, duty, royalty, or annual or periodical payment in money or money's worth, reserved or issuing out of or charged upon land, but does not include mortgage interest; 'rentcharge' includes a fee farm rent; 'fine' includes a premium or foregift and any payment, consideration, or benefit in the nature of a fine, premium or foregift; 'lessor' includes an underlessor and a person deriving title under a lessor or underlessor; and 'lessee' includes an underlessee and a person deriving title under a lessee or underlessee, and 'lease' includes an underlease or other tenancy;

(xxiv) 'Sale' includes an extinguishment of manorial incidents, but in other respects means a sale properly so called;

(xxv) 'Securities' include stocks, funds and shares;

(xxvi) 'Tenant for life,' 'statutory owner,' 'settled land,' 'settlement,' 'vesting deed,' 'subsidiary vesting deed,' 'vesting order,' 'vesting instrument,' 'trust instrument', 'capital money,' and 'trustees of the settlement' have the same meanings as in the Settled Land Act, 1925;

(xxvii) 'Term of years absolute' means a term of years (taking effect either in possession or in reversion whether or not at a rent) with or without impeachment for waste, subject or not to another legal estate, and either certain or liable to determination by notice, re-entry, operation of law, or by a provision for cesser on redemption, or in any other event (other than the dropping of a life, or the determination of a determinable life interest); but does not include any term of years determinable with life or lives or with the cesser of a determinable life interest, nor, if created after the commencement of this Act, a term of years which is not expressed to take effect in possession within twenty-one years after the creation thereof where required by this Act to take effect within that period; and in this definition the expression 'term of years' includes a term for less than a year, or for a year or years and a fraction of a year or from year to year;

(xxviii) 'Trust Corporation' means the Public Trustee of a corporation either appointed by the court in any particular case to be a trustee or entitled by rules made under subsection (3) of section four of the Public Trustee Act, 1906, to act as custodian trustee;

(xxix) 'Trust for sale,' in relation to land, means an immediate binding trust for sale, whether or not exercisable at the request or with the consent of any person, and with or without a power at discretion to postpone the sale; 'trustees for sale' mean the persons (including a personal representative) holding land on trust for sale; and 'power to postpone a sale' means power to postpone in the exercise of a discretion;

(xxx) 'United Kingdom' means Great Britain and Northern Ireland;

(xxxi) 'Will' includes codicil.

. . .

Second Schedule: Part I Covenant implied in a conveyance for valuable consideration, other than a mortgage, by a person who conveys and is expressed to convey as beneficial owner

That, notwithstanding anything by the person who so conveys or anyone through whom he derives title otherwise than by purchase for value . . . the person who so conveys has . . . full power to convey the subject-matter . . . in the manner in which it is expressed to be conveyed . . . and that subject-matter shall remain to and be quietly . . . enjoyed . . . without any lawful interruption . . . by the person who so conveys . . . or by, through or under anyone . . . through whom the person who so conveys derives title . . .

And that, freed and discharged from, or . . . by the person who so conveys, sufficiently indemnified against, all . . . incumbrances as . . . have been or shall be made . . . by any person rightfully claiming . . . through . . . the person who so conveys . . .

And further, that the person who so conveys and any

person . . . having or rightfully claiming any estate or interest in the subject-matter of conveyance . . . by through or under anyone through whom the person who so conveys derives title otherwise than by purchase for value, will, from time to time . . . on the request and at the cost of the person to whom the conveyance is expressed to be made . . . execute . . . all such lawful assurances . . . for . . . more perfectly assuring the subject-matter of the conveyance.

Administration of Estates Act 1925

55 Definitions

In this Act, unless the context otherwise requires, the following expressions have the meanings hereby assigned to them respectively, that is to say:

(1)(i) 'Administration' means, with reference to the real and personal estate of a deceased person, letters of administration, whether general or limited, or with the will annexed or otherwise:

(ii) 'Administrator' means a person to whom administration is granted:

(iii) 'Conveyance' includes a mortgage, charge by way of legal mortgage, lease, assent, vesting, declaration, vesting instrument, disclaimer, release and every other assurance of property or of an interest therein by any instrument, except a will, and 'convey' has a corresponding meaning, and 'disposition' includes a 'conveyance' also a devise bequest and an appointment of property contained in a will, and 'dispose of' has a corresponding meaning:

(iv) 'The Court' means the High Court, and also the County Court, where that court has jurisdiction:

(v) 'Income' includes rents and profits:

(iv) 'Intestate' includes a person who leaves a will but dies intestate as to some beneficial interest in his real or personal estate:

(vii) 'Legal estates' means the estates charges and interests in or over land (subsisting or created at law) which are by statute authorised to subsist or to be created at law; and 'equitable interests' mean all other interests and

178

charges in or over land or in the proceeds of sale thereof:

(viii) 'Lunatic' includes a lunatic whether so found or not, and in relation to a lunatic not so found; and 'defective' includes every person affected by the provisions of section one hundred and sixteen of the Lunacy Act, 1890, as extended by section sixty-four of the Mental Deficiency Act, 1913, and for whose benefit a receiver has been appointed:

(ix) 'Pecuniary legacy' includes an annuity, a general legacy, a demonstrative legacy so far as it is not discharged out of the designated property, and any other general direction by a testator for the payment of money, including all death duties free from which any devise, bequest, or payment is made to take effect:

(x) 'Personal chattels' mean carriages, horses, stable furniture and effects (not used for business purposes), motor cars and accessories (not used for business purposes), garden effects, domestic animals, plate, plated articles, linen, china, glass, books, pictures, prints, furniture, jewellery, articles of household or personal use or ornament, musical and scientific instruments and apparatus, wines, liquors and consumable stores, but do not include any chattels used at the death of the intestate for business purposes nor money or securities for money:

(xi) 'Personal representative' means the executor, original or by representation, or administrator for the time being of a deceased person, and as regards any liability for the payment of death duties includes any person who takes possession of or intermeddles with the property of a deceased person without the authority of the personal representatives or the court, and 'executor' includes a person deemed to be appointed executor as respects settled land:

(xii) 'Possession' includes the receipt of rents and profits or the right to receive the same if any:

(xiii) 'Prescribed' means prescribed by rules of court or by probate rules made pursuant to this Act:

(xiv) 'Probate' means the probate of a will:

(xv) 'Probate Judge'; (Definition substituted by Administration of Justice Act 1970 (c 31). s 1(6) Sch 2 para 5)

(xvi) 'Probate rules' means rules and orders made by the Probate Judge for regulating the procedure and practice of the High Court in regard to non-contentious or common form probate business:

(xvii) 'Property' includes a thing in action and any interest in real or personal property:

(xviii) 'Purchaser' means a lessee, mortgagee or other person who in good faith acquires an interest in property for valuable consideration, also an intending purchaser and 'valuable consideration' includes marriage, but does not include a nominal consideration in money:

(xix) 'Real Estate' save as provided in Part IV of this Act means real estate, including chattels real, by which virtue of Part I of this Act devolves on the personal representative of a deceased person:

(xx) 'Representation' means the probate of a will and administration, and the expression 'taking out representation' refers to the obtaining of the probate of a will or of the grant of administration:

(xxi) 'Rent' includes a rent service or a rentcharge, or other rent, toll, duty, or annual or periodical payment in money or money's worth, issuing out of or charged upon land, but does not include mortgage interest; and 'rentcharge' includes a fee farm rent:

(xxii) 'Rules of Court' include, in relation to non-contentious or common form probate business, probate rules:

(xxiii) 'Securities' include stocks, funds, or shares:

(xxiv) 'Tenant for life,' 'statutory owner,' 'land', 'settled land,' 'settlement,' 'trustees of the settlement,' 'term of years absolute,' 'death duties,' and 'legal mortgage,' have the same meanings as in the Settled Land Act, 1925, and 'entailed interest' and 'charge by way of legal mortgage' have the same meanings as in the Law of Property Act, 1925:

(xxv) 'Treasury solicitor' means the solicitor for the affairs of His Majesty's Treasury, and includes the solicitor for the affairs of the Duchy of Lancaster:

(xxvi) 'Trust corporation' means the public trustee or a corporation either appointed by the court in any particular case to be a trustee or entitled by rules made under subsection (3) of section four of the Public Trustee Act, 1906, to act as custodian trustee:

(xxvii) 'Trust for sale,' in relation to land, means an immediate binding trust for sale, whether or not exercisable at the request or with the consent of any person, and with or without a power at discretion to postpone the sale; and 'power to postpone a sale' means power to postpone in the exercise of a discretion:

(xxviii) 'Will' includes codicil.

(2) References to a child or issue living at the death of any person includes a child or issue en ventre sa mere at the death.

(3) References to the estate of a deceased person include property over which the deceased exercises a general power of appointment (including the statutory power to dispose of entailed interests) by this will.

Family Law Reform Act 1969

1 Reduction of age of majority from 21 to 18

(1) As from the date on which this section comes into force a person shall attain full age on attaining the age of eighteen instead of on attaining the age of twenty-one; and a person shall attain full age on that date if he has then already attained the age of eighteen but not the age of twenty-one.

(2) The foregoing subsection applies for the purposes of any rule of law, and, in the absence of a definition or of any indication of a contrary intention, for the construction of 'full age,' 'infant,' 'minor,' 'minority' and similar expressions in—

    (a) Any statutory provision, whether passed or made before, on or after the date on which this section comes into force; and

    (b) any deed, will or other instrument of whatever nature (not being a statutory provision) made on or after that date.

· · ·

9 Time at which a person attains a particular age

(1) The time at which a person attains a particular age expressed in years shall be the commencement of the relevant anniversary of the date of his birth.

· · ·

14 Right of illegitimate child to succeed on intestacy of parents, and of parents to succeed on intestacy of illegitimate child

(1) Where either parent of an illegitimate child dies intestate as respects all or any of his or her real or personal property,

the illegitimate child or, if he is dead, his issue, shall be benefiting under the disposition or, for the purpose of designating such a person, to someone else to or through whom that person is related; but that subsection does not affect the construction of the word 'heir' or 'heirs' or of any expression which is used to create an entailed interest in real or personal property.

(3) In relation to any disposition made after the coming into force of this section, section 33 of the Trustee Act 1925 (which specifies the trusts implied by a direction that income is to be held on protective trusts for the benefit of any person) shall have effect as if—

    (*a*) the reference to the children or more remote issue of the principal beneficiary included a reference to any illegitimate child of the principal beneficiary and to anyone who would rank as such issue if he, or some other person through whom he is descended from the principal beneficiary, had been born legitimate; and

    (*b*) the reference to the issue of the principal beneficiary included a reference to anyone who would rank as such issue if he, or some other person through whom he is descended from the principal beneficiary, had been born legitimate.

(4) In this section references to an illegitimate child include references to an illegitimate child who is or becomes a legitimated person within the meaning of the Legitimacy Act 1926 or a person recognised by virtue of that Act or at common law as having been legitimated; and in section 3 of that Act—

    (*a*) subsection (1)(*b*) (which relates to the effect of dispositions where a person has been legitimated) shall not apply to a disposition made after the coming into force of this section except as respects any interest in relation to which the disposition refers only to persons who are, or whose relationship is deduced through legitimate persons; and

    (*b*) subsection (2) (which provides that, where the right to any property depends on the relative seniority of the children of any person, legitimated persons shall rank as if born on the date of legitimation) shall not apply in relation to any right conferred by a disposition made after the coming into force of this section unless the terms of the disposition are such that the children whose relative seniority is in question cannot include any illegitimate children who are not either legitimated persons within the meaning of that Act or persons recognised by virtue of that Act as having been legitimated.

(5) Where under any disposition any real or personal property or any interest in such property is limited (whether subject to any preceding limitation or charge or not) in such a way that it would, apart from this section, devolve (as nearly as the law permits) along with a dignity or title of honour, then, whether or not the disposition contains an express reference to the dignity or title of honour, and whether or not the property or some interest in the property may in some event become severed therefrom, nothing in this section shall operate to sever the property or any interest therein from the dignity or title, but the property or interest shall devolve in all respects as if this section had not been enacted.

(6) This section is without prejudice to sections 16 and 17 of the Adoption Act 1958 (which relate to the construction of dispositions in cases of adoption).

(7) There is hereby abolished, as respects dispositions made after the coming into force of this section, any rule of law that a disposition in favour of illegitimate children not in being when the disposition takes effect is void as contrary to public policy.

(8) In this section 'disposition' means a disposition, including an oral disposition, of real or personal property whether inter vivos or by will or codicil; and, notwithstanding any rule of law, a disposition made by will or codicil executed before the date on which this section comes into force shall not be treated for the purposes of this section as made on or after that date by reason only that the will or codicil is confirmed by a codicil executed on or after that date.

Interpretation Act 1978

[Note that much of the act concerns the interpretation of statutes (as will seen by the wording expressly referring to acts) but some sections may have an effect on private documents.]

8 References to distance

In the measurement of any distance for the purposes of an Act, that distance shall, unless the contrary intention appears, be measured in a straight line on a horizontal plane.

9 References to time of day

Subject to section 3 of the Summer Time Act 1972 (construction of references to points of time during the period of summer time), whenever an expression of time occurs in an Act, the time referred to shall, unless it is otherwise specifically stated, be held to be Greenwich mean time.

. . .

17 Repeal and re-enactment

(1) Where an Act repeals a previous enactment and substitutes provisions for the enactment repealed, the repealed enactment remains in force until the substituted provisions come into force.
(2) Where an Act repeals and re-enacts, with or without modification, a previous enactment then, unless the contrary intention appears —
    (a) any reference to any other enactment to the enactment

so repealed shall be construed as a reference to the provision re-enacted;

(b) in so far as any subordinate legislation made or other thing done under the enactment so repealed, or having effect as if so made or done, could have been made or done under the provision re-enacted, it shall have effect as if made or done under that provision.

· · ·

20 Interpretation etc

(1) Where an Act describes or cites a portion of an enactment by referring to words, sections or other parts from or to which (or from and to which) the portion extends, the portion described or cited includes the words, sections or other parts referred to unless the contrary intention appears.

(2) Where an Act refers to an enactment, the reference, unless the contrary intention appears, is a reference to that enactment as amended, and includes a reference thereto as extended or applied, by or under any other enactment, including any other provision of that Act.

Administration of Justice Act 1982

20 Rectification

(1) If a court is satisfied that a will is so expressed that it fails to carry out the testator's intentions, in consequence —
  (a) of a clerical error; or
  (b) of a failure to understand his instructions, it may order that the will shall be rectified so as to carry out his intentions.

21 Interpretation of wills—general rules as to evidence

(1) This section applies to a will —
  (a) in so far as any part of it is meaningless;
  (b) in so far as the language used in any part of it is ambiguous on the face of it;
  (c) in so far as evidence, other than evidence of the testator's intention, shows that the language used in any part of it is ambiguous in the light of the surrounding circumstances.
  (2) In so far as this section applies to a will extrinsic evidence, including evidence of the testator's intention, may be admitted to assist in its interpretation.

22 Presumption as to the effect of gifts to spouse

Except where a contrary intention is shown it shall be presumed that if a testator devises or bequeaths property to his spouse in terms which in themselves would give an absolute interest to the spouse, but by the same instrument purports to give his issue an interest in the same property, the gift to the spouse is absolute notwithstanding the purported gift to the issue.

Bibliography

Austin J L, *How to do Things with Words*, Oxford University Press, 1962

Bede The Venerable, *The Ecclesiastical History of Our Island and Nation*, c 703–735

Chomsky Prof N, *Aspects of the Theory of Syntax*, MIT Press, 1965 Massachusetts; *Cartesian Linguistics: A Chapter in the History of Rationalist Thought*, Harper-Rowe New York and London, 1966; *Language and Mind*, MIT Harcourt Brace Jovanovich Inc New York, 1968, 1972

Clayre A, *Nature and Industrialisation*, Oxford University Press, 1977 (1804)

Engel Sir George, *Statute Law Review*, Spring 1983

Fraser Sir Bruce, *The Complete Plain Words*, Penguin edition 1973, reprinted 1983

Fries Prof CC, *The Structure of English*, Longman, 1952

Gellner E, *Words and Things*, Penguin, 1959

Gowers Sir Ernest, *Fowler's Modern English Usage*, 2nd Ed Oxford University Press, 1965

Herder J G, *On the Origin of Language*, (translated by A Gode) Frederick Ungar Publishing Co New York, 1966

Holdsworth, *History of English Law*, Vols 5 and 6, 1903, 7th Ed 1956

Jespersen O, *A Modern English Grammar on Historical Principles*, George Allen and Unwin London, Ejnor Munksgaard Copenhagen 1954, 1958; *Analytic Syntax*, London 1937

Jones Sir William, *Works of*, (ed) Lord Teignmouth reprinted by J Hatchard, London 1976

Kent Sir Harold, *In On The Act*, MacMillan, 1979

Lewis, Horrabin and Gane, *Flow Charts, Logical Trees and Algorithms for Rules and Regulations*, Civil Service Occasional Papers No 2 HMSO, 1967

Magee B, *Men of Ideas*, BBC Publications, 1978

Murray L, *Grammar in the English Language*, Wilson Spence and Mawman, York (Eng) 1795

Murray J M, *The Problem of Style*, Oxford University Press, 1922
National Consumer Council, *Plain English for Lawyers; Plain Words for Consumers*, 1984
Onions C T, *An Advanced English Syntax*, (published for The Grammatical Society) Routledge and Kegan Paul, 1932
Partridge E, *Usage and Abusage*, Penguin, 1963
Phythian B A, *A Concise Dictionary of Correct English*, Hodder and Stoughton, 1979
Potter Prof S, *Our Language*, Penguin, 1950; *Language in The Modern World*, Penguin, 1960
Rawls J, *A Theory of Justice*, Oxford University Press, 1971
Schlegel F von, *Essay on the Language and Wisdom of the Indians*, (1808) French ed, Paris Parent-Desbarres, 1837
Smith L P, *Words and Idioms*, Constable and Co Ltd, London 1925, 5th ed reprinted 1948
Spencer H, *An Autobiography*, Williams and Norgate, 1904
Strang Prof B, *Modern English Structure*, Edward Arnold 2nd ed, 1968
Sweet H, *New English Grammar, Logical and Historical*, 'Part II: Syntax' Oxford Clarendon Press 1898, 1952
Thring Sir Henry, *Practical Legislation*, HMSO, 1877
Wilson Prof R A, *The Miraculous Birth of Language*, University of Saskatchewan Dent, 1937
Whitten W and Whitaker F, *Good and Bad English*, Newnes, 1939
Wittgenstein L, *Philosophical Investigations*, (translated by G E M Anscombe) Oxford 1953, 2nd ed 1958

Legal Dictionaries

Burke J, *Jowett's Dictionary of English Law*, Sweet and Maxwell, 1977 with supplement
James J S, *Stroud's Judicial Dictionary of Words and Phrases*, Sweet and Maxwell, 1971
Osborne D G, *A Concise Law Dictionary*, 5th ed 1964, Sweet and Maxwell
Saunders J B (ed), *Words and Phrases Judicially Defined*, Butterworths, 1969 with supplement

Index